THE ART OF STORYTELLING
FOR DRAMATIC SCREENPLAYS

BY

JACK W. McADAM

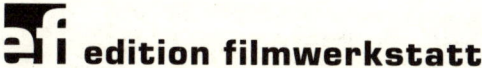
edition filmwerkstatt

IMPRESSUM

e:fi edition filmwerkstatt
Roettgeshof 9
D - 45473 Muelheim, Germany

Permissions may be sought directly from
e:fi edition filmwerkstatt
phone: +49.208.7672603
fax: +49.208.7672604
e-mail: info@edition-filmwerkstatt.de
home: www.edition-filmwerkstatt.de

ISBN-13: 978-3-939596-11-0
ISBN-10: 3-939596-11-6

Graphic design, cover and layout:
Robert Pasitka ℞ www.pasitka.de

Printed and bound in Poland by OPOLGRAF S.A.
www.opolgraf.com.pl

THIS BOOK IS DEDICATED TO
HANS-JOACHIM ESSER–MAMAT,
AT THE INTERNATIONAL FILM, TELEVISION AND
MUSIC ACADEMY (IFFMA) IN GERMANY;
WHERE IT ALL STARTED.

CONTENTS

ACKNOWLEDGEMENTS

THANKS TO THE MANY WRITERS I HAVE WORKED WITH,
WHO HAVE DISCUSSED THEIR WORK AND THEIR IDEAS
WITH ME OVER THE YEARS, HELPING ME TO REFINE MY IDEAS
OF EFFECTIVE STORYTELLING.

AND

THANKS, FOREVER, TO MY WIFE ANNE,
AND OUR DAUGHTER AMANDA, FOR THEIR SUPPORT
AND FINE EDITING SKILLS.

INTRODUCTION

I have been writing for film and television since 1967, and began writing my own original screenplays in the 1990's. I then turned my attention to writing books in 2004, many adapted from my screenplay research.

I have been thinking of writing this book for some time. The idea first began after I presented a series of three-day screenwriting workshops at the International Film, Television & Music Academy in Gauting, Germany, in 1998. I then returned during the summer of 2000. During those lectures, everyone had a story to tell of a real experience or an imagined event, but most had no idea of how to precisely tailor that idea into an engaging screenplay. It was my job to make that possible.

It was later in India, in 2006, when I was invited as the speaker-of-the-evening by the Cinema Peoples Academy in Bombay, India, that a similar writing problem became evident. It seemed to be such a struggle for most filmmakers. Lots of storytellers, but no screenplays of any consequence had been produced. In fact, I was told that many of the local filmmakers would start a film with an idea for a story and simply make it work as they went along without a screenplay, and hope for the best. There should be no reason for this.

A first-rate screenplay is a precise form of storytelling, carefully formatted and timed to meet each dramatic event within a specific framework, with a climactic ending that provides a satisfying and memorable resolution. The following chapters will explore such mechanics with examples of film structures that turn into expressions of story development with character-driven plots. Storytelling is an enjoyable process, turning your story into a screenplay should be the same.

Part One

With me, a story usually begins with a single idea or memory or mental picture. The writing of the story is simply a matter of working up to the moment, to explain why it happened or what caused it to follow.

William Faulkner

Storytelling

So many screenplays, and consequently the actual films that are produced from those screenplays, lack a well told storyline. They seem to start out with great promise but soon flounder from the lack of any dramatic direction to carry the premise. Of all the many faults that contribute to an unsuccessful film it is usually the basic storytelling flaws that appear the most often.

When one thinks of storytelling, the forces of good and evil certainly come to mind. Without that conflict the story lacks the forward motion so important to captivate our imaginations. When we have the opportunity to start at the beginning with a good storyteller our attention will be held throughout that story to the very end. It is only when we reach that final resolution that we, as an audience, can judge the impact of the story on our consciousness.

Some stories will stay with us for days after, especially when they are well told. The images, the characters, and the conflict remain whether we experience those moments on the stage, the screen, or offered by the spoken word when talking to a friend. Film is the celebration from a creative mind, where both the craft of writing and the art of storytelling are carefully combined to produce those special moments of magic.

William Goldman, who wrote such memorable films as "Butch Cassidy and the Sundance Kid" and "All the President's Men," believes that it all comes down to the story. Goldman says, "After writing movies for some thirty-five years, I am more convinced than ever it's only about story."

The Three-Act Structure

Let's start with a dramatic form that your story will usually follow within a three-act structure. You will find the same formula in a Greek tragedy, a five-act Shakespearean play, a four-act dramatic series, or a six-act movie-of-the-week.

In each of these forms we find the basic three-act structure: the beginning, the middle, and the end --- or in other words, the act one **set-up**, the act two **development**, and the act three **resolution** or climax. On the stage, this is more than clear with the curtain coming down at the end of each act.

Television however, because of the commercial breaks, has created a two-act structure for sit-coms, six-acts for a two-hour television movie-of-the-week or in most cases, four-acts for a dramatic series. However, the three-act structure is still to be found in these programs regardless of the artificial act endings created by the interruption of sponsored messages.

Up to now, there are no commercial breaks in a feature film and in most cases you can easily decipher the three-act structure almost to the minute in most films. Of the three act structures, film has the advantage of being highly image-oriented and the set-up of act one in most films begins with **images** to establish a place and a mood, along with the characters that inhabit that setting.

In all three of the dramatic forms, the stage, television or film, one can carefully plot these crucial **turning points** throughout the three acts that will change the lives of our main characters. We place them in or out of jeopardy, turning them into heroes or villains. It is up to us as storytellers to make those decisions. As George M. Cohan once said when discussing a three act structure for the stage: "Get your hero up a tree, throw some rocks at him, then get him down again, it's just that simple." Cohan, of course, had only the stage for such experiments.

When we examine the classic stories written by some of the most acclaimed storytellers in the world, we find the ever-present three-act structure adding momentum and focus to their stories. A number of such storytellers come to mind that have created masterpieces of English and American literature and I have deliberately decided to choose these authors because most of their work has been published worldwide in many languages, and is easily available for further study. They are some of the best storytellers in the business. Any one of them is well worth studying for dramatic style and content.

For this exercise, I selected six of their short stories and divided each story into three-act structures, *without dialogue*. It is just the bare bones of each scene, very much a short **outline** that the writer would use before the final treatment.

In all cases, as I read these stories, the division from one act to the next becomes most evident during this process. As you will see, each story contains interesting characters in the first act set-up. Their actions and decisions brought them to the many dramatic turning points and reversals in the middle story of the second act. Then the third act resolution was played out, completing the story. You will also discover that I have broken down each story into groups of scenes, much like the **beats** we establish in a screenplay outline.

SIX CLASSIC STORYTELLERS

Let's begin with a popular writer of full-out adventure and action stories: Jack London (1876–1916). In the entire history of American literature, no other writer has come close to the worldwide popularity and recognition attained by Jack London, when he was at the top of his profession. Author, sailor, world adventurer, socialist agitator, gold prospector, war correspondent, self-educated scholar, farmer and railroad hobo, all rolled into one great storyteller, all of this before the internet.

Jack London embodied perfectly the lusty, brawling spirit of turn-of-the-century America, the America of the closing frontier and of the last generation of rugged and desperate men who sought their fortune in the wilderness.

His first big success was his novel *The Call of the Wild*, about a dog named Buck who goes from living as a domestic pet to living on its own in the wilderness of Alaska. His most famous short story is *To Build a Fire*, about a man struggling and failing to light a single fire in the snowy wilderness. It is one of the most widely anthologized and translated stories ever written by an American author.

The following Jack London story is titled, *Which Make Men Remember*. It's an excellent example of strong characterization. Make a note of London's use of descriptive adjectives to illuminate the character and illustrate his world. London was also a master at plot twists with ever-changing events that give the story a forward momentum, along with great anticipation for the reader.

* * *

WHICH MAKE MEN REMEMBER

ACT I – (the Set-Up)

In a smoke-filled gambling casino in Dawson City, we find a twenty-two year old boy dressed in a thick scarf and cap. He is unshaven and looks tired as he leans against the bar listening to a group of miners exchanging their stories of adventures in the Klondike wilderness. He is known to his friends as the Malamute Kid. Emil Jensen, one of the miners, seems to be the spokesman for the group. The crowded room is filled with the loud sounds of men drinking and gambling.

Emil offers the Kid a drink and asks him about his future plans. The Kid tells him that he is broke and is trying to hitch a ride back to his home in San Francisco. He admits to the tall miner that after five months of panning for gold on the Henderson River, he came away empty-handed, except for a bad case of scurvy that he can't seem to shake and has been with him for many weeks. Emil says that he can help him with part of his trip, since he is welcome to join him in a few days on his trip south to a port at the Anvik mission. The Kid accepts his friendship with a handshake.

Suddenly a shot rings out, then another, as the casino turns into a riot of men pushing over tables and chairs as they stumble toward the exits. A man is shot in the chest and lying in a pool of blood, as the Northwest Mounted Police arrive.

Outside the casino, a gambler called Fortune Le Pearle appears in the alley and makes his escape into the darkness during a heavy snowfall and hides among the shacks that ring the settlement.

Sometime later, Emil Jensen appears walking towards his shack through the deep snow. Before entering, he notices Le Pearle hiding under a snow-covered canvas and decides to hide him inside his shack. Meanwhile, an angry search party carrying lighted torches sweeps through the settlement loudly shouting their displeasure.

Act II — (the Development)

During the daylight hours, Emil hides the gambler under a section of the floorboards as the police continue a search through the settlement from door to door. At night, however, Le Pearle emerges to play games of solitaire, "like a man possessed by the devil." The cards and the luck of the draw mesmerize him. Within a few days, the search for him ends and everything goes back to normal.

Le Pearle thanks Emil for helping him to escape, he is indebted to him. Emil surprises Le Pearle by suggesting that he will take him along on his trip south to the mission at Anvik. It is a steamship port on the Yukon River, and once onboard the paddle wheeler he would be able to escape to freedom. Le Pearle agrees and offers to pay Emil for his kindness, but the miner will not take payment.

Early the next morning, just before sunrise, Emil, the Malamute Kid and Le Pearle quickly pack their belongings and the food rations and slip away by dog-team into the frozen wasteland.

For five days and nights they travel with the Kid needing to sometimes travel on the sled as his legs are stiff with scurvy and he can only shuffle through the snow for short periods of time. On these painful occasions Emil helps the young man and the two become close friends.

When they camp at night and build a fire, Le Pearle continues to play out a hand of solitaire before falling asleep. Emil also notices that the gambler is carrying a small pearl-handled revolver, which he occasionally checks and cleans before returning it to his vest pocket with much care.

On the fifth morning, they are within a day of the mission at Anvik and freedom for La Pearle. He is anxious to get on with the trip and is the first one to rise as the Kid builds a fire.

As Emil prepares breakfast over the morning campfire, he tells Le Pearle that the man he murdered at the gambling table was one of his mining partners. His name was John Randolph, Emil's blood brother and an honest man.

The old miner tells him that he has waited all this time for justice to be done! Before Le Pearle can react, the old miner grabs his gun and holds it against his head. Emil has decided to beat Le Pearle at his own game. He will give him a gambling opportunity, something that John Randolph never had. They will play a game of 'chance' with the same revolver that Le Pearle killed Randolph with. Le Pearle has no choice but to agree as the Kid looks on.

ACT III – (the Resolution)

The Kid holds a deck of cards as the two men make a 'high-card' draw for first choice. Emil draws a king-of-hearts, but Le Pearle wins with an ace-of-spades.

Le Pearle paces out fifty-feet, then turns, aims his revolver and fires at Emil. The shot is wide. The kid retrieves the gun and hands it to the old miner. Emil reloads the gun and takes his turn.

The shot drops Le Pearle right in his tracks, as the loud sound reverberates along the snow-encrusted ridge.

Suddenly, an avalanche of snow breaks away and proceeds to bury Le Pearle, the dog-team and all of the supplies. Just as quickly, Emil pulls the Kid clear of the cascading wall of ice and snow, as both men are pitched down the mountainside.

By the luck of the Irish, the Kid and Emil are miraculously swept clear of tons of snow and ice that narrowly miss them. The bodies of Le Pearle, the dog-team and all of their supplies are lost from sight, forever.

However, Emil is still left with his compass and half-a-bottle of whiskey. Once clear of the avalanche, Emil and the Kid climb back onto the ridge and find their direction, as they head off across the frozen wasteland. The Kid at this point can hardly walk and Emil helps him.

Sometime later, they emerge from the tree line and gaze down at the river valley. In the distance, they see the chimney smoke from the mission settlement at Anvik, drifting across the distant landscape. They are elated and move forward with Emil still helping the Kid with every painful step. They will survive after all. God is good.

* * * THE END * * *

It has been reported that Jack London was a great fan of Rudyard Kipling and that he studied the fine craft of dramatic writing by copying, line for line, Kipling's very popular animal stories published in his *Jungle Books*. Soon after the publications, Kipling was awarded the Nobel Prize for Literature.

I should also add an interesting irony. After traveling the world for a few years, Kipling finally settled in the State of Vermont. And it was there, in a rented cottage surrounded by the snow, that he began to reimagine the India of his childhood, and wrote the book that he is best known for today, *The Jungle Book*.

The motion picture, *The Man Who Would Be King*, starring Sean Connery and Michael Caine and directed by John Huston, is one of Kipling's famous short stories that has become a classic film for all ages. This film is well worth studying for the fine development of character, and especially for the final tragic flaws dramatically revealed in the third and final act.

The following story, *The Most Dangerous Game*, by Richard Connell (1893–1949) received the prestigious O. Henry Memorial Award. It is a life-or-death adventure story set in a very exotic place, the Amazon basin of South America. This particular set of circumstances is based on the most popular type of conflicts in dramatic writing -- **man against man**.

In this case, our main character has a very definite goal, but another character stands in his way, preventing him from reaching that goal. He is ready to lay down his life, if need be, just to secure one thing and one thing only --- his sense of personal dignity. It's a story as old as *The Epic of Gilgamesh*, one of the oldest surviving tales.

* * *

THE MOST DANGEROUS GAME

ACT I – (the Set-Up)

Sanford Rainsford, a very rich industrialist and celebrated big game hunter, author and world traveler, has a fascination for exploring the most challenging countries in his hunt for big game. While visiting at the Explorers Club in Los Angeles, Rainsford hears of the black jaguars of the Amazon. Within days he is heading on his private yacht down the Atlantic coastline in search of this animal.

Once onboard he tells his companions of his hunting exploits around the world, and in all of these exploits he has never been satisfied with the challenge of his quarry. Lions and rhinos in Africa, the great polar bears of the Arctic, the Bengal tigers in India or the wild boars found in the dense jungles of Borneo, have not satisfied his lust for adventure.

One moonless night, while cruising at the mouth of the Amazon River, he hears gunshots from the distant shoreline. In his enthusiasm to seek out the direction of the gunfire, he stumbles at the rail and falls overboard into the dark water.

Unbeknown to his companions or crew, Rainsford is soon lost in the wash of the speeding yacht. His calls for assistance are lost in the night. He is able to somehow swim through the darkness and finally drags himself onto a rocky shoreline, exhausted, but glad to be alive.

Again he hears shots, possibly pistol shots, the sounds of barking dogs and the anguished sounds of a hunted animal coming from the darkened jungle beyond. Rainsford is both fascinated and concerned for his predicament as he stumbles along the dark shoreline listening for further sounds, but there are none.

At the base of a cliff, he climbs an outcropping and settles down for the night in the branches of a large tree. The night is silent around him; only the crashing surf is heard as he falls asleep, exhausted but confident that he will survive his ordeal.

ACT II – (the Development)

In the morning, in the first rays of the sun, he climbs a cliff and enters the dense jungle. As he continues through the jungle he is suddenly aware of the silence around him. There are no birds or animals to be seen or heard.

He soon finds an animal path and follows it. The path circles a swamp, filled with quicksand and tall grasses. Rainsford, with his jungle experience, recognizes the danger and circles the area before rejoining the path.

Sometime later he finds the distinct print of hunting boots that lead him out of the dense jungle and along a section of cliff that overlooks the ocean. He surmises that he is on a narrow island as he continues along the cliff. At the end of the island, to his great astonishment, he comes upon a palatial chateau high on the cliff overlooking the sea.

As he approaches the grounds, a pack of dogs in a nearby kennel compound sees him and begins barking. Rainsford ignores them and makes his way up the path toward the building.

At the massive front door an athletic looking man greets him dressed as a Russian Cossack. He introduces himself as General Yuri Zarkoff and welcomes him. Once inside, his kindness is overwhelming as he directs his servant to find clothes for Rainsford immediately.

Rainsford is then shown to a guest room in the large chateau, where he is able to take a bath and clean up before joining the General for dinner in the large banquet room. The Russian feeds him in grand style, with serving after serving of fine cuisines and exotic wines.

Then he brings a book out of his library and explains that he is most honored to have such a famous author and big game hunter visit him at this time. He believes fate has finally brought the two men together. Having read all of Rainsford's books, he has become a great fan of his ingenuity and daring as a hunter. The General tells Rainsford that he is going to meet his most dangerous and elusive combatant.

Later that evening as Rainsford retires to his room, he is sure that he hears the cries of human voices coming from the depths of the chateau, somewhere in the very foundations. Early the following morning, Rainsford is awakened by the General's valet and given hunting clothes, a backpack of food rations, a knife and a pair of moccasins. He is told to dress and join the General in the main hall.

ACT III − (the Resolution)

Over breakfast, Rainsford soon finds out that he is on an island that is owned by the General who also considers himself a great hunter and keeps a game preserve. However, he soon finds out that the old General's sport is hunting the human survivors that are ship wrecked on his island and he keeps them locked up under the chateau in the vaults.

Rainsford is appalled by this and both men have a heated debate on such an immoral act as using humans for the hunting pleasures of the General. The General suggests that it is the ultimate hunting experience; only man has all the instincts including the intellect for such a life-threatening encounter.

The General makes a challenge to Rainsford. He will hunt him over six nights, and if Rainsford, with his famous hunting instincts, can outmaneuver the General, then he will be free to leave the island. Rainsford suggests that if he is successful he wants the shipwrecked survivors to be released also. The smug General agrees to such a deal and they shake hands.

After breakfast Rainsford is led into the jungle and told that he has the rest of the day to hide. The hunt will begin at sunset and end at sunrise, no earlier and no later. That night, under the bright light of a full moon, the Cossack General pursues his quarry, pistol in hand. He looks for footprints, but finds none, no evidence of broken plants or other telltale signs of Rainsford.

Night after night the human hunt continues, much to the delight of the crazed Cossack. Hunting dogs, death traps, pits and quicksand all became part of the hunt, as Rainsford and the General play their macabre game of life or death in the island jungle.

Finally, nights later, Rainsford, now bruised and beaten, slowly circles back around the island undetected and carefully makes his way into the chateau, just before sunset. In his bedchamber, the General loses the hunt. Rainsford steps out of the shadows and quietly claims his victory.

* * * THE END * * *

The following story, *The Fourth Man*, by John Russell (1912–1982) is a perfect example of a story that is truly **character-driven**. Establish three escaping convicts, with little value for life, along with a native at the helm of a homemade reed-boat, set them adrift in the Coral Sea and you create a seemingly impossible dramatic situation. The uncomplicated **plot** is survival, but fate, as usual, has already predetermined the result of this little escapade.

You can almost hear the explosive dialogue exchanges between these desperate men as you read this outline. In this situation the unforgiving sea around them becomes as important as their will to survive for another day.

* * *

THE FOURTH MAN

ACT I – (the Set-Up)

The figures of three desperate men can be seen moving through a jungle on the French island of New Caledonia. It is daybreak; the jungle is dense and mist-covered. When they reach a path that leads down to the Pacific ocean, we see for the first time that they are dressed in ragged and dirty striped convict clothing.

At the water's edge a dark-skinned Canaque native meets them. After a brief introduction he leads them to a desolate alcove and they board a long reed boat, which he has built. He directs them to help as they push it through the shallows. Once clear of the reef, the men board and the craft heads out to sea in the first light.

The three men look apprehensively back at the island. They have been planning this escape from the penal colony for the past year and finally the day has come. They smile at each other as they continue to paddle, while the native sits at the stern and guides the long reed boat with a tiller.

Doctor Dubosc, a large man with a full beard, is the most dangerous of the three convicts. Fenayrou, an Iranian rug salesman in his former life, is the most depraved, while Perroquet, a short wiry man who wears a pair of thick glasses, is the one convict with the official reputation of escaping the most times from the penal colony and being recaptured.

None of them knows the sea and all feel uncomfortable in the flimsy cane raft except the native, who sits crouched at the stern steering the small vessel. The three men continue to paddle for all of the morning until they are exhausted.

By the afternoon, the small boat enters the warm currents of the Coral Sea, as the men try to protect themselves from the searing sunshine and sleep through the heat. The native sits at the tiller and hums to himself, completely at ease with the environment and the hot sun overhead.

ACT II — (the Development)

That night the water is jealously divided in a thimble-like container between the three of them. The men ignore the native as they share their meager ration of cigarettes. We learn that the Doctor has made an arrangement for a freighter to pick them up and take them to Australia, which happens to be some eight hundred miles away.

With the native able to guide the boat by the stars at night, they decide it's best to paddle at night and rest through the hot days. This seems to work for the first few nights, but as the hours and the days go by, exhausted and hungry, they begin to fight among themselves unsure that they will ever board the freighter.

Then they squabble over the cigarettes and lose most of them overboard while engaged in a bloody fistfight. They have an argument over the last of the water and spill a great portion of it before they ever get to drink it. That very night they are blessed by a torrential rainfall, but the small boat is tossed back and forth in the grip of the storm, completely awash with the pounding seas.

Lightning and thunder fill the sky. But they are too exhausted and seasick to try and collect the heaven-sent rain as it runs away into the reed meshing of the boat.

Early the next morning, Fenayrou gets into an argument with Doctor Dubosc. He blames him for not making a better arrangement with the freighter that is supposed to pick them up. Why is it so late? Did Dubosc really make an arrangement, or was this his way of getting them to help him escape? Fenayrou attacks him and calls him a liar and a cheat and the Doctor smashes him across the head with his paddle in an angry rage. Perroquet tries to separate them.

That evening Perroquet suspects that the native is hiding food and water and they attack him. Fenayrou threatens him with his knife, and then beats him but to no avail. The native simply ignores their pleas and returns to his world of quietly gazing at the stars, while he guides the boat toward Australia.

Later that night, while the other two are sleeping, Perroquet wakes up with a fever. He talks to himself and becomes entranced with the reflection of the moon on the water.

At one point, weak and delirious he tries to crawl overboard into the shark-infested ocean. The native pulls him back at the last moment and saves his life, unbeknown to him.

The convicts are beyond themselves. They can't sleep during the day or the night for fear of treachery and they no longer have the strength or the desire to even paddle the reed boat.

When the catamaran is in a calm, they can only rely on the current and the native to set a course. The Doctor assures Fenayrou and Perroquet that the boat will come, he believes that with all his heart. The other men have no reaction. They are completely beyond hope of surviving.

ACT III — (the Resolution)

Finally they fight over the last of the water. Doctor Dubosc takes the water container away from Fenayrou and proceeds to finish it. Fenayrou in a rage knifes Dubosc. The Doctor dies at the feet of Perroquet, who is too weak from fever to understand. The native watches from the stern of the homemade boat without any reaction to the killing.

Some days later, onboard the freighter "Ulysses", Captain Jean Guilbert sights the catamaran on the horizon and sets his course towards it. As he pulls alongside he sees the convicts stretched out in the bottom. He recognizes the Doctor, once an associate of his. Upon a further examination he discovers all three are dead.

The Captain introduces himself to the native and explains that a series of storms at sea held back his progress. His crew lifts the three bodies of the convicts off the boat and prepare a burial-at-sea.

The native appears to be in good health however, and tells the captain that he wants to return home to his family. The Captain wishes him well as he leaves. Once onboard, the native spreads his own sail of pandanus leaves and heads the catamaran back toward the island of New Caledonia.

Moments later, he takes a hollow reed with a sharp end and, stretching himself to full length in his accustomed place at the stern, he thrusts the reed down into one of the storage bladders that he had installed under his raft and drinks his fill of the sweet water. Then the native casually sits back at the tiller and softly hums to himself as a light breeze tugs at the sail.

* * * THE END * * *

The next story is *Wine on the Desert* by Max Brand (1892–1944). Brand was one of the most prolific authors of all time, with over 500 novels and short stories published; yet he heartily disliked the West. However, here is one of his classic western stories, and like most of his stories, this storyteller explores the depths of human nature with **character-driven** plots. This is a simple study of a man's revenge, and as it soon turns out, it's both ironic and life threatening.

A simple **theme** as this can easily be expanded into more than two characters. What would happen if the protagonist in this story had a sidekick or two? How would that shape the end of the story? What if there was more at stake?

When I think of such story possibilities it brings to mind, *Treasure of the Sierra Madre*. This bleak adventurous motion picture was shot on a desert location, very similar to the location in this story. The film starred Humphrey Bogart and Oscar winner Walter Huston, brilliantly directed by John Huston, who also won an Oscar for this 1948 black-and-white classic. Check it out; it's a very powerful tale.

* * *

WINE ON THE DESERT

ACT I – (the Set-Up)

Dick Durante is a cowboy on the move. He has been riding for the last several hours, every now and then stopping near a high ridge to look back, checking to see if he can see anyone following. There doesn't seem to be, but he appears nervous and anxious to arrive at his next location somewhere over the scraggy-covered hills.

Sometime later, he shades his eyes against the hot noon sun as he searches the hills. Finally he finds it. He sees a rancher's windmill beyond the next rise, and quickly rides toward it.

After he tops the last rise, he rides down into the hollow, past the ten acres of lush vines and passes a score of tanks made of cheap corrugated iron. Slender pipelines carry the water from the twenty tanks to the vines and from time to time let them sip enough life to keep them, until the winter brings new rains.

Durante has only visited the ranch in the rainy season; he has never been here during the drought. It is hot and dry. The grapes had been gathered, the new wine had been made, and now the leaves hang in ragged tatters.

He throws the reins of his mule aside and strides into the house. He is in the process of drinking his fill of water from a kitchen water cooler, when he hears the wooden leg of Tony bumping on the floor; they meet with a friendly handshake. Tony's wife is in town visiting her sister for a week. Durante decides to rest from the long ride in a hammock, while Tony prepares dinner.

Over a meal of tortillas and a young rabbit, they drink Tony's wine and talk about life. Tony's father built the vineyard and set up the well to supply the water-tanks with water for the vines. Without the storage water, the vineyard would die.

He pours Durante his father's wine, eleven years old, he is very proud of this wine. Tony describes how his father died in the desert. There was a leak in his canteen. Without a supply of water on the desert you're a goner --- "my father was only five miles away when the buzzards showed him to me."

ACT II – (the Development)

The next morning, Durante is awakened by the sound of a single gunshot, and then Tony appears holding a rabbit by the ears, the rifle in his other hand. He tells Durante that if he catches them in the sights, they are dead. There was a neat hole right through the head. A shudder goes down the back of Durante as he washes gingerly before breakfast, feeling his blood cooled for the entire day.

It is a good breakfast of flapjacks, stewed rabbit with green peppers along with a quart of strong coffee. The hot sun shining through the east window starts the two men sweating as they finish eating.

Durante asks to look at Tony's rifle. Tony hands him the fifteen-shot Winchester, and tells him to take a look, but don't steal the luck that's in it and laughs. Durante takes the loaded rifle and calmly commands Tony to step outside.

Then he tells Tony to step away where he can see him. Then he tells him that the sheriff will be coming along this trail sometime today looking for him. He'll load up himself and all his gang with water out of your tanks, and then he'll follow my signs across the desert looking for me. Durante then says that the sheriff will follow only if he finds water on the place, but he's not gonna find water here and waves the rifle toward the tanks.

Tony pleads with him. He tells Durante that he could hide him in the old wine cellar. Durante shakes his head, puts the rifle to his shoulder, aims and fires. The shot strikes the base of the nearest tank and a semicircle of darkness begins to stain the soil near the edge of the iron wall. Tony falls on his knees and pleads. The vineyard will die. Durante continues to drill bullet holes through the tanks, one after another. Tony falls on his face and puts his hands over his ears; he cannot look at what is happening.

When he has finished, Durante prods Tony with the empty rifle and tells him to take his canteen into the house and fill it with water from the kitchen water cooler.

Tony gets up slowly. He raises the canteen and looks around him, not at the tanks from which the water is pouring so that the noise of the earth drinking is audible, but at the rows of his vineyard. Then he goes into the house.

Durante mounts his mule. He shifts the rifle to his left hand and draws out the heavy Colt from his holster. When Tony returns, he gives up the canteen without lifting his eyes or without saying a word to Durante.

Durante takes it and scorns him. 'The trouble with you, Tony, is you're yellow. I'd of fought a tribe of wildcats with my bare hands before I'd let 'em do what I'm doin' to you.' Then Durante shakes the canteen to make sure it is full, kicks his mule into a dogtrot and leaves the ranch.

ACT III – (the Resolution)

About half a mile from Tony's ranch he throws the empty rifle to the ground. There's no sense packing that useless weight, and Tony with his peg leg would hardly come this far.

Durante looks back, a mile or so later, and sees the little image of Tony picking up the rifle from the dust, then staring earnestly after his guest. Durante remembers the neat little hole clipped through the head of the rabbit.

Wherever he goes, this trail never could return again to the vineyard in the desert. But then, commencing to picture to himself the arrival of the sweating sheriff and his posse at the ranch, Durante laughs heartily and kicks his mule forward.

Durante pats the full, rounding side of his canteen. He might even now begin with the first sip but it is a luxury to postpone pleasure until his desire becomes greater.

Sometime later, he raises his eyes along the trail. The Apache Desert stretches in front of him like an unbroken chalk-line, pointing toward the cool blue promise of mountains on the distant horizon. The next morning he would be among them he boasts to his mule as they continue toward the mountains.

Hours go by. He looks at his watch, it is only ten o'clock, and he had thought that it was on the verge of noon! Suddenly, a coyote whisks out of a gully and runs like a gray puff of dust on the wind, his tongue hanging out like a little red rag from the side of his mouth.

Durante is dry to the marrow, but he has waited for this moment. He carefully uncorks, lifts his canteen and swallows a great mouthful before his senses could give him warning. It's wine!

Durante has to somehow survive the next twenty-four hours not on water but wine. He must go on and somehow win through. Once he turns the mule and considers the return trip, but remembers the head of the rabbit, drilled right through the center.

The day grows old. Nausea is beginning to work in Durante's stomach, nausea alternating with sharp pains. When he looks down, he sees blood on his boots. He has been spurring the mule at a gallop for a long time.

The mule does not die until after sunset. Durante leaves everything except his revolver. He carries it for an hour or two, and then discards it into the sand, tossing it aside, without looking back.

He seizes his shirt at the throat and tear it away so that it hangs in two rags from his hips and stumbles across the rocks before he falls for the last time face down, then slowly rolls over onto his back.

There are no stars in the heavens, he is blind. Durante hears the sand blowing over him. After many hours, a cool rain begins to fall, as the big birds find their way down to one place in the desert.

* * * THE END * * *

The next example was not written as a short story, but I decided to take it as an episode from Stephen Crane's novel, *The Red Badge of Courage*. As a writer, Stephen Crane (1871–1900) was a brilliant impressionist and certainly one of the founders of American realism. His method of writing soon became known as "naturalism" in which his characters would face very realistic and often bleak circumstances. He was also the author of two books of poetry. Crane had a brief adventurous life as a war correspondent in Cuba and Greece and unfortunately died of tuberculosis at the young age of twenty-eight.

Crane had no war experience when he first wrote this American masterpiece, but he created almost a poetic fable about the attempt of a young man to discover his real identity in a battle, in this case, the American Civil War. Take note of his excellent ability to capture the very essence of the useless turmoil of war.

Here is another example of a story that could take place in any of the wars since then. Only the names of the characters and the locations change, but human nature when faced with the senseless tragedy of war remains the same. Just look at the daily news on television or in our newspapers for that stark reality.

* * *

THE RED BADGE OF COURAGE

ACT I – (the Set-Up)

One night in 1862, as young Henry Fleming lay in his bed, the winds had carried to him the clamoring of the church bell to tell the news of a great battle. This voice of the people rejoicing in the night had made him shiver in a prolonged ecstasy of excitement.

Later that week, early one morning, he had gone to his mother's bedroom and told her that he was going to enlist. She told him not to be such a fool and sadly covered her head with a quilt on her bed.

Nevertheless, the following morning Henry went to the small town that was near his mother's farm and enlisted in a company that was forming there and signed up with other young men.

Back at the farm, he packed his clothes, kissed his mother and left. Still when he looked back at the gate, he had seen his mother kneeling among the potato parings. Her brown face, upraised in prayer, was stained with tears. Henry bows his head and leaves, feeling suddenly ashamed of his purpose.

However, on the way to Washington his spirit soared. The regiment was fed and caressed at station after station until the youth had believed he must be a hero. Then came the many months of monotonous life in a camp. Henry had had the belief that real war was a series of death struggles with small time in between for sleep and meals. Then one morning, that all changed as they formed ranks and marched off.

After a number of days, they reached their destination and the column broke into regimental units and set their tents. Then one night, they formed columns and left. They marched for hours, crossing two pontoon bridges. Hours later, they climbed a hill as artillery began to boom, marched forward into a woods and right into a skirmish. Explosions and musket fire surrounded them.

He began to feel the effects of the war atmosphere, a blistering sweat, and a sensation that his eyeballs were about to crack like hot stones. A burning roar filled his ears. Men dropped here and there like bundles. The youth turned to look behind him; he was alone in hell. A large explosion shook the earth.

ACT II − (the Development)

The youth awakened slowly. Dazed from the onslaught, he picked up his cap from the ground. It was over at last! The supreme trial had been passed and he was still alive. There were some handshaking and deep speeches with men whose features were familiar, but with whom the youth now felt the bonds of tied hearts. He helped a cursing comrade to bind a wound.

Suddenly the shells, which had ceased to trouble the regiment for a time, came swirling again, exploding in the grass and the trees. The youth stared. Surely, he thought, this impossible thing was not about to happen again, but the enemy's fire only increased into a raging onslaught. His comrades began to fall on all sides, while others scampered away through the smoke.

He too, threw down his gun and fled. There was no shame in his face. He ran like a rabbit, as he began to speed toward the rear in great leaps. The youth went on, moderating his pace since he had left the place of noises. He overheard a soldier report to the general that their line held. The youth cringed as if discovered in a crime. By heavens, they had won after all! He could hear cheering. He turned away amazed and angry and felt that he had been wronged. He left from the fields into a woods as if resolved to bury himself.

Once he found himself almost in the middle of a swamp. At length he reached a place where the high, curved boughs made an arch. Then he stopped horror-stricken. He was being looked at by a dead soldier, over the gray skin of the face ran little ants. The youth turned and fled into a nearby stand of trees.

He finally came to a road from which he could see in the distance dark and agitated bodies of troops. The wounded men were cursing, groaning and wailing as he joined the staggering procession. A tattered soldier with half-an-arm asked the youth where he was wounded. He fell back in the procession until the tattered soldier was not in sight, wishing that he too had a wound of some sort, a red badge of courage to show to his comrades.

In this line of wounded and dying soldiers, the youth met his old friend Jim, who was badly wounded and half-crazed with pain. The youth was determined to help him and although the tall soldier pleaded to be left alone, Henry was determined to help him.

Sometime later, writhing in agony, Jim died in his arms. The youth found himself climbing a fence and he wandered through a field away from the fallen body of his comrade. Then as he rounded a hillock he looked down on a roadway now a crying mass of wagons, teams and hundreds of men in retreat.

ACT III — (the Resolution)

Instead of joining the retreat, he wanted to head back to the front. A certain moth-like quality within him kept him in the vicinity of the battle. So when he saw a column of stalwart replacements marching toward the front lines he wanted to join them. He told himself that, despite his unprecedented suffering; he had never lost his greed for a victory, the sooner the better.

Suddenly he saw a dark wave of men that swept out of the woods, and behind them blue smoke curled and clouded above the treetops. The fight was soon lost and Henry found himself in the midst of the battle. A man turned in a lurid rage and swung his rifle butt against the youth's head and he sank writhing to the damp ground. Pressing his hands to his temples he went lurching across the grass, as the blue haze of evening quickly closed upon the field.

That night he found his old company in the nearby woods. The corporal took a handkerchief and wrapped it around his wound. He was given a blanket and was soon in a deep sleep next to the smoldering campfire in a quiet wooded setting.

The next morning his regiment was marched to relieve a command that had lain long in some damp trenches and the youth took his position behind a curving line of rifle pits. The cannons were roaring without an instant's pause for breath. He moved forward with the regiment and soon they were advancing into the woods full of smoke and explosions.

The color sergeant was killed and the youth took the flag from him and urged the men forward. His regiment bustled forth with undiminished fierceness into the battle, through the smoke and the cannon fire that erupted from all sides.

So it came to pass that as he trudged from the place of blood and wrath his soul changed. It suddenly started to rain heavily. The procession of weary soldiers after the battle soon became a bedraggled train, both despondent and muttering with lifeless steps.

Yet the youth smiled, for he saw that the world was a world for him, though many discovered it to be made of oaths and walking sticks, Henry was determined to survive and boldly marched on.

∗ ∗ ∗ THE END ∗ ∗ ∗

Charles Edward Montague (1867–1928) was an English journalist and a writer of novels and essays. In 1915 he became an armed escort for VIPs visiting the World War I battlefields. He escorted such personalities as H. G. Wells and George Bernard Shaw into the trenches on one occasion to review the war. His story called *Action* certainly has some effective twists and turns, but ends up with a gratifying, exciting ending. So many times a writer may have his ending to a story well before he plots the beginning; this could be just such an example of that.

If the **plot** carries the action in this story, then surely the **sub-plot** carries the theme of self-preservation --- finding one's self and regaining the spirit for life. Here is a story that could take place anywhere, in any time frame that you may choose --- the storyteller can even take us to a different locale, but the basic plot will always remain the same.

∗ ∗ ∗

ACTION

ACT I – (the Set-Up)

Christopher Bell, the president of a large insurance company, is fifty-two years old today and his employees have thrown him a surprise birthday party. Bell is given a number of presents, while he drinks and dances away the evening.

Later that night he is chauffeured home, feeling no pain, and enters his apartment. The doorman tells him that the elevators are not working and apologizes for the inconvenience. Bell shrugs, he jokes that such a climb is nothing for a mountaineer like him and begins to quickly climb the stairs two by two. On the ninth floor, exhausted and weary, he unlocks his door and enters his penthouse. Alone now without his wife, who passed away some years earlier, Bell pours a nightcap and carries his drink out onto his private patio that overlooks the sprawling city below.

Suddenly, he suffers an enormous rush of pain down his right side and grabs at the railing; as the dazzling lights of the city revolve before his eyes, he slowly and painfully sinks to his knees.

Sometime later, his physician arrives and after an examination tells Bell that he has experienced a mild stroke. This could be the first indication of a heart problem. His doctor suggests that he should have a thorough examination. After that he should not return to his office but plan a period of rest and relaxation, maybe at a vacation spot away from the city.

The next morning Bell wakes up to find that the sensation in his arm is still there; he has trouble completely closing his right hand. He feels very depressed over his condition as he slips out of bed. Bell looks at a picture of his deceased wife. She is wearing a ski outfit and they are together standing on a chateau patio in the Swiss Alps. Both are smiling in a warm embrace and much in love.

Bell picks up the telephone and dials a number. He tells his office he is leaving town for a week or so, he'll keep in touch and hangs up with a determined look on his face. His life is about to change forever.

ACT II − (the Development)

That afternoon finds Bell on an airplane to Switzerland. He has his briefcase beside him and is busy putting his legal papers in order, including his final will and a letter to determine the transfer of his stock and bonds in his corporation.

Sometime later he arrives in a little summer hotel in the Rhone Valley. It is September; the end of the tourist season, and Bell is alone except for the widow Gaspard, an elderly woman who is left to maintain the hotel and to prepare for the winter season. They happen to be old friends and she is pleased to see Bell, but curious that he has unexpectedly arrived at this time of the season, with practically no one in the hotel.

Bell tells her that he had a sudden urge to retrace the joys of his boyhood and the many years of a happy marriage. He wanted to return to an old familiar vacation spot in the Swiss mountains that brought him so much pleasure.

As old friends, they talk of bygone days when the four of them, husbands and wives, would go mountain climbing and complete the *Grande course*. They both enjoy the memories, the dangerous moments on the mountains, the companionship they shared, and their years of true friendship.

Early the next morning, unbeknown to anyone, Bell slips away from the hotel fully dressed and carrying the necessary equipment to begin what he considers his last climb. He spends part of the morning climbing the grass covered slopes, then some time later he crosses the lowest dip of the stately Weisshorn, at 12,000 feet high, with a noticeable chill in the air.

Bell soon enters the ice field and begins to cut his way forward up the steep face toward the Schallihorn. He attacks the steepest face and slowly begins to cut his ice ladder of footholds almost vertically all the way to the ridge high above. He now works with a determined effort, much like he once did as a young man many years before.

His right hand begins to tingle once more; he blindly pushes on, trying to ignore the condition. Bell is exhilarated; his face is covered in perspiration as he continues the difficult climb.

Some hours later, as the sun begins to set, he finds himself immobile under an outcropping of sheer ice. Bell is totally exhausted, and his hands are becoming numb from the cold. His left hand and arm have lost all feeling. He clings precariously to the face of the mountain. He cannot go on. Far below, the setting sun sends long shadows across a mist-covered valley.

Bell is on the edge of becoming unconscious, a state that he welcomes. If he must commit suicide, this was his choice, his finest hour. The mountain will soon claim another brave soul.

Bell watches the distant sunset rim the mountaintop sending flares of light across the wind-swept patches of drifting snow far above him and forces a smile at the magnificent scene. This will be his last image of life on earth.

Act III − (the Resolution)

Suddenly an ice ax bounces off the wall of ice beside him, narrowly misses his head and disappears into the twilight below. Bell looks up to see a young woman in distress. She is hanging on a line connected to her husband above who is pinned against the glacier and can't move. The woman has lost her footing and is swaying free on her safety line.

Bell shouts his instructions to the two climbers. He tells them not to move, he is on his way. Finding strength he didn't know he had, Bell cuts and climbs very slowly around the outcropping of ice toward the woman.

He finally moves to her side and secures her rescue. Then very slowly and carefully he cuts his way up the glacier with her. Bell reaches her husband and leads them to safety. They are overwhelmed by his bravery as the trio hug each other on the top of the ice shelf, happy to be alive.

Sometime later, under the light from a full moon, the trio are able to take refuge in an old Weisshorn hut. A fire is lit and they enjoy their food rations while discussing their harrowing life-and-death experience, and they become good friends.

Bell now realizes that by arranging a rescue for both of them, he saved himself. For some strange reason he has regained the strength and feeling in his right arm. It was all psychosomatic.

The following morning, the sky is clear, the bright sunshine shimmers across the majestic mountains that surround them, as they step outside. Bell admits to the young couple that he was depressed and planning suicide when he began his climb. But that has all changed now, thanks to them.

The three of them now make their way carefully down the mountain, with Bell confidently leading the way. Through this experience, Bell has regained his faith in humanity and his spirit for life has returned.

* * * THE END * * *

As you can see I enjoy action adventure stories, especially when the storyteller takes his characters off to exotic and unusual destinations. The stories that you have just read are examples from great storytellers. Each writer had a definite idea of how they wanted to structure their story, the time frame, the place and the characters that occupy that space. Good and evil is presented, a hero or a villain is revealed and eventually dealt with, as we turn the final pages to the end.

In literature there are many ways to express such stories on the written page. However, when that story is created for film, the basic plot may remain the same, but the characters, the setting and the mood of the story are refined into an image-orientated series of pictures. And the writer is no longer alone. His creation is eventually joined and retold by actors, a director, a cinematographer, and a company of creative talent that all have their own interpretation of his story. It becomes a new language, reshaped and sometimes exploited for the public to see. As Jean-Luc Godard once said, *'Film is reality in twenty four frames per second.'*

In the following chapters we will explore such elements of effective storytelling for the screen. Some of the information is very basic, but what I have introduced here, for your consideration, is a completed action-adventure screenplay worked up from the inspiration for the story, to the outline, to the finished first draft, with notations and specific storytelling observations on each of the major scenes. It is a novel approach, in the true sense, for the creation of a motion picture story.

PART TWO

A WRITER'S PROBLEM DOES NOT CHANGE. HE HIMSELF
CHANGES AND THE WORLD HE LIVES IN CHANGES BUT
HIS PROBLEM REMAINS THE SAME. IT IS ALWAYS HOW TO
WRITE TRULY AND HAVING FOUND WHAT IS TRUE,
TO PROJECT IT IN SUCH A WAY THAT IT BECOMES A PART
OF THE EXPERIENCE OF THE PERSON THAT READS IT.

ERNEST HEMINGWAY

Plotting the Story

I recall taking a master writing class with Syd Field in the 1980's, in Hollywood, where we examined the structure that he saw at work in a successful screenplay, especially one that sold. It was Syd that coined the word **paradigm** in reference to a basic approach to the structure of a screenplay. In the philosophy of science, a paradigm is a model of how ideas relate to one another, to form a conceptual framework. Syd defined the three acts, with the addition of specific plot points in the action, and how the major conflicts were resolved, all using this simple formula. I'm sure I still have a photocopy, somewhere in my writing files, of Syd's hand-drawn diagram explaining his paradigm structure and how to apply it.

Syd introduced us to plot points, midpoints, and time frames, but it was Aristotle who introduced us to the three-act structure, over 2,500 years ago. Aristotle was a student of Plato and a teacher of Alexander the Great, and among other things, he taught him the basic elements of drama. Here is what he said. "It should have for its subject a single action, whole and complete, with a beginning, a middle, and an end. It will thus resemble a living organism in all its unity, and produce the pleasure proper to it." And it appears we have followed his advice ever since.

Let's proceed with our three-act structure, that you have just read in these six short stories, a step further. We should be able to fit any one of these stories into a one hundred and twenty page screenplay. Considering that each page plays approximately one minute of film, you would end up close to one hundred and twenty minutes of screen time, a desirable length for motion picture exhibitors to be attracted to the picture, not to mention a producer that has to sell it.

A familiar method for many writers, for plotting the three acts and to time the length of each act, is the use of a series of 3"x5" cards laid out in vertical rows of three cards each. This means that the first THREE cards will determine the **first act**. The next SIX cards become the **second act**, and the last THREE cards, the **third act**. It is similar to a step outline, used by many writers, but the cards make it more convenient to shuffle your scenes, if that is necessary.

Each card should contain around ten minutes of material, something that you can time when you play the film in your head, as you write the scenes on the card to cover that length of time. When you have reached the end of the third card, you have played thirty minutes of screen time, and so on, as you continue with each card blocking the timed scenes.

The first act cards (which contain the Set-Up), should establish the world, the characters, the reason for them being in the story and a major plot point (from pages 25 to 27) that thrusts both your protagonist and antagonist into the second act with a new direction, new needs, a momentum with possible twists.

The second act cards (the Development), number six with a total of sixty minutes of screen time. Continue to plot each card to be approximately ten minutes each, and again end with a major plot point (from pages 85 to 90). This act, according to most writers, is sometimes the toughest, being the longest of the three acts, while sustaining your story direction and keeping a lifeline between the two acts.

The third act, or climax of the film, consists of three cards, each ten minutes of screen time with the final resolution usually occurring in the last ten minutes or so in your story. Here is an approximate page count for the three acts.

ACT I	ACT II	ACT III
Set-Up	Development	Resolution
page 1 to 25	page 25 to 90	page 90 to 120

In many cases, the final twists in the plot are more interesting when the writer creates a false ending, then discloses a final ending that delivers an ending unique, uplifting and memorable. Look at any of the classic film endings that come to mind and you will appreciate such creative storytelling.

THE ONE-PAGE STORY SYNOPSIS

Let's begin our story concept with a short **synopsis**. This should be the nuts and bolts of your story, told as briefly as possible, and usually never much longer than one page. In most cases a few well-structured paragraphs to sum up your idea is effective. I chose one of my screenplays for the following synopsis titled:

THE PRINCE OF RUSSIA

This is a 1993 sea adventure about Mark Fletcher, an eighteen-year-old boy who travels with his father to Russia. Mark decides to visit Nikolai, his grandfather, while his father proceeds to conduct deep-sea dive trials for a Russian Admiral with a sophisticated dive suit called the Newtsuit, which he developed with his research company.

34

The grandfather, being an old hard-hat salvage diver, takes Mark on a treasure dive in the Baltic Sea to find The Prince of Russia, a World War II freighter that is reported to hold a large shipment of American gold. Nikolai's tugboat is mysteriously sabotaged, before their dive happens, by an unknown assailant and they barely save themselves. They desperately beach the sinking tugboat at the last moment, just before entering the harbor, but all is lost.

Determined to save Nikolai's salvage business from bankruptcy, Mark arranges to steal one of his father's dive suits, and a Russian dive boat, unbeknown to Nikolai. He is now able to return to the location to find the treasure. Through a series of life-or-death circumstances, Mark finally reaches the freighter, but accidentally stumbles onto a sunken German U-boat. When his Newtsuit springs a leak he is able to miraculously save himself by entering the dry portion of the submarine through an escape chamber.

However, he is now trapped with no means of reaching the surface and with little air left to breathe. His father and Nikolai soon arrive on the scene and desperately combine forces, the old with the new. They rescue Mark by incredibly refloating the sunken U-boat.

Unbeknown to anyone, except the young adventurer, they find a fortune onboard the submarine. Nikolai is now rich beyond his wildest dreams and Mark becomes the hero of the land.

Or if you had to boil this idea down to a short **pitch** for a producer it would read:

This is a thrilling action/adventure story that takes place just after the fall of the Soviet Union. Set against the rugged coastline of the Baltic Sea and on the ocean floor off St. Petersburg, The Prince of Russia is a story of a corrupt naval admiral and his assassin bent on murder, during a heroic offshore rescue. It is a sensitive drama of a young man's discovery of love in a foreign land, undaunted loyalties and discovered relationships, set against the explosive, unyielding cruelty of the sea.

Or if you were asked for a **log line**, in twenty-five words or less, just edit your pitch down for something like this:

An epic story of incredible acts of courage and betrayal, young love and murder, where the sea brings down all but the strongest.

This synopsis was created by myself and Robert Landry, who was my partner on this story. We first worked together when I was the Production Designer on a 70mm. underwater adventure film, produced by Sandy Howard, for 20th-Century Fox titled, *The Neptune Factor*. Bob was our underwater specialist and master diver who supervised the many underwater action sequences in our dive tanks in Toronto, and on the open sea in Halifax, Miami, and in the Bahamas.

It was Bob's background and diving knowledge that gave our story such a realistic edge. He has been on many professional treasure and salvage dives over the years, and still continues today. Bob introduced me to the revolutionary diving system called the *Newtsuit*, designed and developed by Dr. Phil Nuytten. This is a lightweight atmospheric dive suit that can accomplish effective work at depths of 305 meters. Bob had worked with this suit during diving tests in Vancouver.

However, the original **idea** for this story, was not at all what you just read in this synopsis. Our story, at that time, was based on a small marine salvage yard near Halifax, Nova Scotia. We had a plan for a treasure dive for gold near Bermuda, possibly on an 18th century Spanish privateer, such as the Mark Antonio, that was wrecked in 1777. Both of us as experienced divers knew these locations well. So the initial concept and our research for the sites were based on these locations; that is, until I happened to come across the following *Reuter News* item published in the *Los Angeles Times*, and it changed everything!

CZARIST TREASURE STILL HIDDEN?

MOSCOW (Reuter) The Amber Chamber, a czarist treasure seized by Nazis and lost since 1945, is hidden underground in a German bunker, a most recent report claims.

A Soviet newspaper said the bunker complex was built for Adolph Hitler. Rabochaya Trubuna said the treasure is below what later became a Soviet military base at Ohrdruf in the eastern German state of Thuringia. Soviet troops stationed at the base never investigated the 45-metre-deep galleries of "Hitler's buried capital and storehouse."

The newspaper said it was still constrained from publishing any documents in its possession, which might prove where the treasure was hidden.

```
The treasure is a priceless collection of amber wall
panels, furniture and other amber artifacts. Among
the clues was a receipt for transporting 126 boxes
from Koenigsberg, in 1945 the capital of German East
Prussia, but now the Soviet city of Kaliningrad.
That's where the treasure was last displayed.

The receipt for the collection was found after World
War II in a German kitbag belonging to an SS officer
helping to evacuate the works of art.
```

That small news item put a completely different spin on the story for me. Our 18th century gold in the Bahamas suddenly became the Tzar's lost amber treasure in the 20th century, during the occupation of the German Army. The story location for the salvage yard in Halifax now became the port of Tallinn, on the Baltic Sea, with a Russian navel academy in St. Petersburg. Because of the nature of the story during the war, I conveniently added a German U-boat for added suspense.

The rest of the necessary research for those particular locations quickly followed. Our characters remained the same; they were simply different nationalities in a very different country. The story also became much larger in scope, both on an international level and certainly on a political one, since the collapse of the Soviet Union in January of 1992. I also took advantage of that historic event by setting our story in June of 1993, right on the coattails of such political chaos.

THE SCREENPLAY OUTLINE

Now let's go back to the three-act outline using the **synopsis**, that you just read. Based on that synopsis here is the original outline for the *Prince of Russia* screenplay, carefully plotted on twelve cards, and constructed in three acts.

You may also note that all essential information to the crew, especially the cinematographer and the properties department, are presented in CAPS. This is a traditional application that may be found in all shooting scripts. I like to include that information in my outlines; it helps me focus on the objects in the scenes, including the important items within the action.

* * *

The Prince of Russia

Act One – Card #1 – (the Set-Up)

FADE IN:

AN UNDERWATER SCENE

as shafts of sunlight refract in all directions. We hear the SOUNDS of controlled breathing through diving regulators as the two DIVERS suddenly enter the scene. The first diver, MARK FLETCHER, is followed by ANATOLI TSARKOV.

Just below them a large sunken FREIGHTER looms large in the fading light as they slowly descend and enter the open cargo HATCH and disappear.

INSIDE THE CARGO HOLD

Mark leads the way through a maze of collapsed deck beams to a jagged hole in the hull. He moves through the opening followed by Anatoli just as an outgoing crosscurrent hits. His suit is ripped and he is sent reeling through the opening.

Having seen what happened to Mark, Anatoli calculates the flow of the current and makes his move. He is almost clear, but the reverse current catches him. It slams him into the hull. His REGULATOR is yanked free and he can't reach it.

Terror fills his eyes. He can't hold his breath much longer. Suddenly, an arm shoots through the opening. Mark frees his regulator and pulls him out.

Swept clear of the current, the two divers 'buddy-breathe' toward the surface until Anatoli untangles his regulator.

ON THE OCEAN SURFACE

they board a Boston WHALER. Anatoli is still in shock. He thanks Mark for saving his life. Mark says he owes him one, as the boat heads toward the harbor.

Mark needs to meet his father for a demo on a revolutionary dive suit called the 'Newtsuit' and a Russian Admiral who is interested in purchasing these suits.

They enter the harbor and dock beside a group of research vessels all bearing the International Center for Ocean Research (ICOR) Dolphin insignia.

INSIDE THE ICOR LOBBY

a receptionist tells Mark that he is very late for the demo and his father has been looking for him. She hands him a LETTER. Mark smiles at the postmark.

INSIDE THE LAB TANK ROOM

they walk toward an 80,000 gallon TEST TANK in the middle of the room. Technicians
are dressed in white lab coats working on various projects. Anatoli tells Mark that he
must change into his Russian uniform for the demo.

INSIDE A DARK BOARDROOM AT ICOR

two MEN view a rupture test on a Newtsuit, but all the tests fail beyond 200 feet. The
chief engineer tells DR. IAN FLETCHER that the fault is with the shoulder seals.
They need three more weeks to come up with a new design.

Fletcher says they haven't got that kind of time. He angrily tells him that he is not
going to lose a sale to the Russians. Without this sale the company is bankrupt. He
tells him to destroy the videotape and to come up with a new design.

INSIDE THE TANK ROOM

Anatoli returns and joins Admiral YURI KOCHINKO who is impressed by a DIVER,
in the tank, in his yellow Newtsuit. Fletcher directs the diver in a series of maneuvers.
At the conclusion, Mark joins his father, and he meets the Admiral.

The Admiral learns that Mark's dead mother was Russian, born in the Estonian town
of Tallinn. The Admiral is pleased Mark will be traveling with his father to Russia
for test dives in the Baltic Sea. He will see them on the plane and leaves.

ACT ONE – CARD #2

Now alone with his father, Mark says he got another letter from his grandfather, and
he is going to join him on a treasure dive, rather than work with his father. Nikolai
found a freighter called *The Prince of Russia* loaded with gold ingots.

Fletcher tells him it was sunk over sixty years ago; someone has found the gold by now.
They argue and Mark tells his father that Nikolai needs his help more than Fletcher
does. Fletcher tells him that he is as foolish as Nikolai, and walks away.

ON THE AEROFLOT JET

Mark and Anatoli are playing chess. The Admiral and Fletcher are reviewing their preparations for test dives with the Newtsuit. Anatoli will lab test the second Newtsuit at the Naval Yard in St. Petersburg. Fletcher says he needs more time. The Admiral agrees, he can make use of his time with a training program for his Russian crew. They toast with vodka. The Admiral calls his photographer to take pictures of the successful partnership as he orders more vodka.

The Admiral learns that Mark will not be working with his dad. He will join his grandfather on a treasure dive on a WWII freighter that he found. The Admiral appears interested, since he was in the last days of the war as a young sailor.

Fletcher says that it was carrying an American gold shipment. The Admiral asks if he recalls the name. When Fletcher tells him it was *The Prince of Russia*, the Admiral is highly agitated but hides his reaction from Fletcher.

As the jet prepares to land in St. Petersburg, the Admiral's photographer appears to say that the Admiral would like a photograph of Mark and Anatoli. They agree and the photographer takes a couple of pictures.

AT THE AIRPORT

Anatoli is met by his cousin KALIN, whom he introduces to Mark. When Mark tells her that he is taking the train to Tallinn to visit his grandfather, she tells him that she happens to live there. Mark is obviously taken by her.

THAT EVENING IN THE ADMIRAL'S RESIDENCE

the Admiral is meeting with the Economic Chairman of the Promstroibank. We learn that these two men were involved in stealing the gold on the freighter, when it was sinking, then had all the records destroyed. They are the only living survivors.

The Admiral says if Nikolai dives on the site it will open new investigations, but he has a plan to get rid of him. Special Forces Lieutenant BORIS GORZENKO arrives and gets his instructions. They know he'll resolve matters in his own way.

THE NEXT AFTERNOON

finds Mark on a train that winds through the seaside settlements. Hours later he arrives at the Tallinn railroad station. He looks for a familiar face in the crowd.

BORIS GORZENKO

checks a PHOTO of Mark and Anatoli that was taken on the plane. He spots Mark who is met by SERGEI KOZLOV, Nikolai's partner in the salvage business. Sergei takes him to his truck and leaves. Gorzenko follows the truck in his black Volvo.

ACT ONE – CARD #3

SERGEI'S TRUCK

drives through the town square of Tallinn and past an ancient fortress. Sergei recounts the time four years ago, when Mark first visited his grandfather, and they raced each other up the fortress stairway to the top of the tower.

SOMETIME LATER

they arrive at Nikolai's salvage yard and park beside a refitted TUG BOAT called the *Baltic Star*. Meanwhile, Gorzenko's Volvo stops just outside the gate. He watches them with a pair of binoculars as they board Nikolai's tugboat.

INSIDE THE BARGE GALLEY

Mark is excited to see Nikolai and they hug each other. Nikolai says that Fletcher called and he is still very unhappy that Mark is not with him, but Mark remains indifferent. He is really looking forward to the treasure dive with Nikolai.

LATER THAT NIGHT

they celebrate after dinner with a *tanzi*, an Estonian drinking horn filled with Tsinandali wine, while they tell Mark about the dive site. It is a wonderful evening and Mark feels very much at home with both men.

MEANWHILE ONBOARD THE BALTIC STAR

Gorzenko enters the engine room and goes directly to the main SEACOCK. He checks the connections to the diesel with his flashlight, then climbs under the frame and begins to work on the flange that holds the seacock.

SOMETIME LATER

Mark and Nikolai stagger up the gangplank, just as Gorzenko leaves the engine room. Nikolai challenges him. Gorzenko knocks him aside and when Mark tries to stop him he karate chops him and disappears into the night.

THAT EVENING ONBOARD THE R.V.NORDENSKIØD

the Russian research vessel, Fletcher is on the phone with Nikolai. He is sorry he missed Mark but he must be tired from the trip. They discuss the new diving equipment that Nikolai wants to buy when his bank loan is cleared.

ON THE STERN DECK

a HELICOPTER lands with the Admiral. Fletcher takes him to the stern deck to see the Newtsuit preparations for the dive. The Admiral asks Fletcher when the *Baltic Star* sails. Fletcher is surprised that he knows the name of Nikolai's tug.

THE FOLLOWING MORNING ON THE BALTIC STAR

Mark wakes to the SOUND of rivets being replaced right above his bunk. He staggers out on deck. Nikolai and Sergei are reinforcing a loading crane. They talk of the assailant last night. Sergei says he checked the tug and nothing is amiss.

SOMETIME LATER

TULCHINSKY from the Promstroibank arrives to meet with Nikolai. Nikolai is shocked that the bank will not extend his credit. They plan to liquidate all his assets. Tulchinsky leaves. Nikolai plans to leave for the dive site immediately.

ACT TWO – CARD #4 – (the Development)

LATER THAT MORNING

Mark is helping Sergei make the final repairs to the diesel engine, while Nikolai is on the deck busy patching his antiquated hard-hat DIVING SUIT. A phone call is taken by Sergei who playfully tells Mark that it's a woman, with a very sexy voice.

EARLY THAT EVENING

finds Mark in his cabin neatly dressed in a sport jacket and slacks looking very debonair. He is going on a date with Kalin. He practices his Russian in a nearby mirror. The SOUND of Sergei's truck horn is heard and he rushes out.

SERGEI'S TRUCK ON THE COASTAL HIGHWAY

at SUNSET, as Mark continues to knot his tie. He practices his Russian on Sergei, but Sergei surprises him with the fact that she most likely prefers to speak Estonian. They enter Tallinn and the truck stops in front of a BOOKSTORE.

INSIDE THE BOOKSTORE

the smoky interior is crowded, listening to a YOUNG MAN reciting poetry. It is a poem about the lure of the sea. Kalin meets Mark and tells him that she needs to run an errand. In the alleyway, Kalin loads books into her car and they drive off.

SOMETIME LATER

They arrive at Peter the Great's summer PALACE. In the library she tells him of her childhood in Ottawa. Her diplomatic father left her mother and they returned to Tallinn. In the ballroom they enjoy a picnic and romantically dance together.

KALIN'S CAR

arrives back at Nikolai's dry-dock, just before SUNRISE. Kalin gives Mark a TALISMAN of Baltic amber, for good luck. They kiss tenderly and she drives off. Mark is on cloud nine and bounces up the tug's gangplank.

Act Two – Card #5

THAT MORNING ON THE BALTIC STAR

the tug steams toward the dive site. They are confident of finding gold on the old freighter. As they are ready to dive, they receive a MAYDAY from a burning boat. Nikolai gives up the gold to save the fishermen and leaves at full-steam.

Meanwhile, down in the engine room, three of the five bolts securing the main seacock have been CUT IN HALF by Gorzenko, and now begins to move under the strain. A spray of seawater starts to fill the space under the throbbing diesel.

THE BURNING FISHING BOAT

is sighted and the tug pulls alongside in heavy seas. Sergei and Mark manage to pull four survivors out of the water. Mark recognizes one of the dead fishermen as the young man who was reading poetry in Kalin's bookstore. He is shocked. One fisherman remains on board fighting the fire. As his strength fails he tries to board the tug and falls into the sea. Mark dives in and saves him just as the fishing boat explodes. The tug pulls away with SMOKE from their engine room.

IN THE ENGINE ROOM

Sergei finds the area flooded and tries to fix the flange. It is an impossible task. He talks to Nikolai and they turn toward home as the tug continues to flood. Then without warning the SEACOCK explodes. Sergei and Mark quickly exit the room.

Act Two – Card #6

They have no choice but to run the tugboat onto the beach. The collision causes Nikolai two cracked ribs. An ambulance takes him. Kalin meets Mark and Sergei and they wade ashore. Gorzenko is in the crowd, pleased to see the beached tug.

LATER THAT NIGHT

Mark and Kalin are on the beach near the tug. Mark tells her that Nikolai has returned from the hospital. He is feeling fine but disappointed that he lost everything. It is a romantic night as they walk the beach and board the tug.

THE NEXT MORNING

in the tugboat's cabin Kalin and Mark wake up to the SOUNDS of trucks and a bull-dozer. When they step outside they are met by Tulchinsky with a crew and equipment to refloat the old tugboat, and have the bank claim it for salvage.

Mark is outraged by his attitude and they get into a political argument, cheered on by the crew. Mark finally grabs his NEW SUIT and knocks Tulchinsky down. After they leave, Mark has an idea inspired by Kalin. They need Sergei right away.

ACT TWO – CARD #7

SERGEI'S TRUCK ON THE COASTAL HIGHWAY

Mark explains to Kalin and Sergei that Anatoli has agreed to let them have a dive boat and the extra new suit as long as he can join them. They will find the gold and surprise Nik. They arrive at the Naval Yard and are met by Anatoli.

ONBOARD THE R.V. ANASTASIA

the ultra-modern research vessel heads to the dive site. Anatoli proudly shows them the latest electronic equipment. In the wheelhouse, Anatoli gives the Russian helms-man instructions. It is GORZENKO, unbeknown to anyone.

ACT TWO – CARD #8

AT THE DIVE LOCATION

Mark steps into the Newtsuit and is lowered into the sea. In the WHEELHOUSE, Gorzenko changes into a survival outfit from his uniform. He arms himself with a pistol and a knife, and smashes the ship telephone.

MEANWHILE ON THE RUSSIAN SHIP

Fletcher receives a report that Anatoli has taken a dive boat and the Newtsuit. He calls Nik and admits that this suit was not refitted with the new seals and will likely rupture beyond 200 feet. Nikolai is angry. It may cost him Mark's life.

Nikolai tells him the exact coordinates for the site and they decide to meet there as quickly as possible. Nik will travel in his workboat, along with his hard-hat equipment, and Fletcher will arrive by helicopter. They hope they are not too late.

ON THE DIVE SITE

Mark successfully descends onto the deck of THE PRINCE OF RUSSIA. The old freighter is hanging precariously over the edge of a deep ABYSS. The current is strong and he has to hang onto the railing as he enters the ship's companionway.

Once inside, with Sergei giving him directions from a plan of the ship, he soon finds the treasure room. He levers open the rusty unlocked door and cautiously enters the small space. He spots the four CHESTS that contain the gold ingots.

IN THE WHEELHOUSE

Gorzenko opens a briefcase, which contains eight packs of plastic EXPLOSIVES. He carefully connects each of the wires to an electronic TIMER. He closes the case and exits the wheelhouse, with the briefcase, toward the engine room.

ACT TWO – CARD #9

MEANWHILE NIKOLAI

struggles to keep control of the wheel on his workboat. It squats low in the water from the weight of a large COMPRESSOR. On a ship-to-shore radio he talks to Fletcher who has just lifted off. He tells Nik the *Anastasia* is not receiving.

MARK USES HIS MANIPULATORS

to force open one of the four CHESTS, which puts pressure on the shoulder seals. When the silt settles his light reveals an EMPTY container. The other three chests are also empty. Mark is devastated, so are the trio onboard the *Anastasia*.

AT THE WINCH CONTROLS

Sergei begins to retrieve the UMBILICAL, when he notices the engine room door swinging close. Being suspicious he tells Anatoli to take over. He goes to the room and finds Gorzenko switching on the timer for the explosives in his briefcase.

Sergei confronts him and there is a fight. Gorzenko pulls his pistol in the struggle and fires, narrowly missing Sergei. Gorzenko then knocks him out with the pistol butt. Gorzenko sets the explosion for five minutes and quickly exits the room.

GORZENKO

steps onto the deck and is met by Anatoli. They fight each other. Anatoli is chopped across the head and falls. Sergei lunges out of the hatchway with the BRIEFCASE and rams it into Gorzenko, knocking his pistol across the deck. When Sergei swings the case at Gorzenko's head he deflects it and it is sent flying OVERBOARD. When Gorzenko climbs the rail Anatoli attacks him. He pulls his knife to kill Anatoli, but is SHOT twice and falls overboard. Kalin holds his pistol.

MEANWHILE MARK

is now on the stern deck ready for his ascent. The briefcase hits the deck, unseen by him, and slides overboard. A moment later, a tremendous EXPLOSION rocks the freighter. The impact knocks Mark off his feet and he falls off the deck.

MARK

picks himself up on the seabed, beside the towering freighter. He shines his LIGHT into the darkness. In the swirling sand his light reveals the conning tower of a German SUBMARINE. He tells Sergei of his find and they are all astonished.

ON THE DECK OF THE U-BOAT

Mark finds a hatch. He playfully pulls on it and it opens. Sergei cautions him when he wants to enter it. He says he only needs a few minutes. Sergei reluctantly agrees. Mark disconnects his umbilical and drops out of sight into the chamber.

NIKOLAI NOW ARRIVES IN HIS WORKBOAT

and boards the Anastasia. He is told that Mark has entered a U-boat after disconnecting his umbilical and they have lost communication. Nikolai is angry. He grabs his HARD-HAT equipment and begins suiting up with Sergei's help.

INSIDE THE SUBMARINE CHAMBER

Mark discovers he is in a large four-man ESCAPE chamber. When he reaches above his head his arm unexpectedly locks into position. It takes all his strength to pull it back down causing the shoulder SEAL to suddenly RUPTURE.

A spray of freezing seawater enters his suit, FLOODING him. He has no choice but to close the hatch to make a seal. He then opens the discharge valve, all the while holding his breath, as the seawater fills his suit. It soon engulfs his FACE.

ACT THREE – CARD #10 – (the Resolution)

ONBOARD THE ANASTASIA

Nikolai and Sergei are working feverishly with the antiquated gear in preparation for the dive. Nikolai is struggling with the dive suit, his ribs giving him pain with every movement. Fletcher's helicopter now appears and lands on the deck pad.

IN THE ESCAPE CHAMBER

Mark blows one of his high-pressure auxiliary AIR TANKS and the water drops around him leaving a dry chamber. He unlocks the separation lever to release the water. He climbs out of the suit, gasping for breath, but glad to be alive.

FLETCHER

joins Nikolai and learns of Mark's predicament. When he sees Nikolai in the final stages of suiting up with cracked ribs he stops him. He says he is in no shape for the dive. He feels responsible for Mark's situation and is going to take the dive.

MARK

unlocks a HATCH and descends a ladder into a large compartment. His light reveals racks of grease-covered TORPEDOES and bunks below the racks filled with skeletons. He turns away from the awful reality of the scene around him.

MEANWHILE A DIVE PLATFORM

with flood lights and a video camera descends toward the wreckage, with Fletcher at the rail. Bubbles trail from the exhaust valve on his helmet. Anatoli tells him that he gave him an audio coupler if he needs to communicate with Mark.

BACK AT THE DIVE STATION

Anatoli reports that the Department of Naval Records just reported on the telex that the U-3037 was the latest type XXI Class U-boat. It went to sea in 1945. But what is very strange, they can't find any records of it ever being in the Baltic Sea.

MEANWHILE MARK ENTERS THE CONTROL ROOM

and his flashlight reveals a SKELETON at the chart table wearing a Commander's hat. When he looks at the chart it shows they were on their way to Sweden, a neutral country, before the sub sank. Mark is shivering and feeling dizzy.

FLETCHER ON THE DIVE PLATFORM

sights the U-boat and lands on the deck. He sights Mark's umbilical and confirms that Mark has entered the submarine. Sergei tells him to be careful, the explosion has fractured the drop-off, it could collapse. The sub shifts and Fletcher holds on.

INSIDE THE SUBMARINE

Mark is hurled across the compartment and slowly struggles to his feet in a daze, it's difficult to breath. Suddenly he hears the distinctive tapping SOUNDS on the hull. He grabs a fire extinguisher and taps back three times, thrilled with hope.

ON THE DECK OF THE SUBMARINE

Fletcher hears the reply and announces that Mark is alive. They are delighted at Dive Control. Fletcher wants a torch, he will cut him out. Nikolai says they don't have the time. Fletcher is already into a long decompression and they argue.

Sergei comes up with the idea of blowing the ballast and bringing the submarine up to the surface on its own. Fletcher agrees and Nikolai sends him an airline to attach to the sub's external salvage coupling, just under the anchor hatch.

MEANWHILE MARK

is increasingly unsteady on his feet for lack of good air. He staggers to the center of the compartment waiting and listening for more signals. Suddenly the loud SOUND of escaping AIR explodes into the submarine's ballast tank.

AT THE BOW OF THE SUBMARINE

Fletcher watches in horror as the AIR erupts from the side vents in a continuous cloud of ESCAPING air-bubbles.

AT THE DIVE STATION

Fletcher's voice is heard over the speaker. The air is bypassing the tanks; the bypass valve must still be open. Anatoli tells him to mount the audio coupler onto the hull. They need to talk to Mark, and see if he can close the valve himself.

MOMENTS LATER INSIDE THE SUBMARINE

Mark is surprised to hear Sergei's echoing VOICE with instructions on the bypass lever. He finds it frozen with age. He slams the fire extinguisher against it and the lever drops. The sub takes on a new SOUND as air fills the ballast tanks.

AT THE DIVE STATION

they watch the monitor as the sub begins to shift, then begins to rise, slowly at the stern. Suddenly, the seismic monitor begins to jump again. Nikolai shouts at Fletcher to clear the submarine but his warning is drowned out with static.

FLETCHER

is immediately thrown off balance with the seismic tremor from under the sub as the rising U-boat violently rolls in response to the refilling of the ballast tanks.

THE OLD FREIGHTER

begins to slip nearer to the edge of the drop-off, as debris and cables tangle with the submarine. A tow cable snags across the deck. It instantly slices Fletcher's AIR HOSE and he collapses. Air bubbles explode from his severed umbilical hose.

ACT THREE – CARD #12

THE PRINCE OF RUSSIA

continues to slowly slip forward, then it drops off the ridge into the DEEP. The submarine continues to slowly float upwards, now clear of all cables and debris.

INSIDE THE SUBMARINE

Mark staggers into a wardroom full of trunks and crates. His light illuminates a macabre scene. Six skeletons are at a table playing poker. Stacks of priceless AMBER surround them. On a chair he sees the coat-of-arms of Peter the Great.

AT THE DIVE STATION

the group watch the monitor in horror. Fletcher is lost in the swirling cloud of silt and sand as the great gray shape of the U-3037 fills the screen on its way to the SURFACE. Nikolai and Kalin rush to the starboard rail in eager anticipation.

THE SEA BESIDE THE ANASTASIA

as the submarine breaks skyward, before dropping onto the surface. The trio are alongside in a ZODIAC and board the U-boat. They find Fletcher still alive with his umbilical snagged on a cable. They rush him to the decompression chamber.

ON THE CONNING TOWER

Mark exits and meets Kalin. She is overcome with emotion and they kiss tenderly.

SOMETIME LATER ON THE ANASTASIA

Mark talks to his father through the porthole of the decompression chamber. Mark now realizes that it was his father who saved his life, and for the first time in a long time they smile at each other. It is a new beginning for both.

LATER THAT DAY

Anatoli shows Mark the photograph and notebook that they found in Gorzenko's bag that was left in the wheelhouse. It proves without a doubt that the Admiral covered up the fact that he took the gold shipment and destroyed the evidence.

JUST AT THAT MOMENT A SIKORSKY HELICOPTER

lands on the deck. The Admiral appears with his pilot carrying an UZI. He tells them that he is taking charge and they are under arrest for jeopardizing a military mission. Anatoli says that Gorzenko is dead and they have proof he took the gold.

The Admiral's face flushes with anger and he tells the pilot to shoot them all. Sergei suddenly appears from behind the pilot with Gorzenko's gun to his head. Nikolai quickly steps forward and floors the Admiral with a powerful uppercut.

SOMETIME LATER THIS STRANGE ARMADA

approaches Tallinn with the Anastasia in the lead. Nikolai's workboat has the U-boat in tow. A radio broadcast is heard from the tug's wheelhouse with the news of the German U-boat and the discovery of Tzar Peter the Great's lost treasure.

MARK AND KALIN

stand on the BOW holding hands as a flotilla of small boats and pleasure crafts converge on the group all blowing their horns and whistles in a wild celebration.

THE BALTIC SEA

as the menacing silhouette of the U-3037 passes through the bright reflections of a Baltic sunset, just as it did on a similar summer evening some 52 years earlier.

FADE OUT.

* * * The End * * *

This outline is 12 pages in length, using the card method, and includes every scene in the screenplay. Outlines can run from 10 to 25 pages; however, it really depends on what satisfies your story sense and how much detail you want to include in this breakdown on each card.

Some writers, once they've written a synopsis along with a completed outline, feel they've said it all, and the screenplay becomes anticlimactic for them at that point. If that is so, then there is something wrong with their outline. It may be too detailed, and the writer has fallen in love with his first ideas.

I can't wait to get onto the screenplay to further explore the characters with **dialogue**. They become alive for the first time, transformed into speaking roles, and they begin to take on their own personalities and special traits because of that. This is usually when your muse joins the party, if not earlier, and everyone has his or her own opinions, which you need to deal with. You need to watch those inner voices, they're not always right, and could lead your story astray.

When you have carefully covered all the scenes in your outline and you have all of your story research in line, you should be able to write an excellent first draft screenplay in a very short five weeks. I simply transfer my outline pages into a separate file on my iMac, adding or deleting the outline description as I create, write, and explore the dialogue for each scene.

Honest dialogue will enhance the conflict and explore the inner workings of your character, while always moving the story forward. Where they live and how they live is a good indication of who they are. Most actors try to replicate in real life the emotional conditions under which their character operates, in an effort to create a life-like, realistic performance. So add the odd prop, for the future actor or actress in your story to work with, a cane, a pipe, eyeglasses, hats, a talisman, even the foods they prefer adds dimension. You have created their world with dialogue and placed them in scenes, so enhance them with characteristics and the odd habit that helps to explore their personalities. Method acting is still popular.

The most important thing to remember, at this point, is to press ahead with your dialogue from scene to scene, all the while creating that spoken and unspoken energy between your various characters. Try not to go back and rewrite, regardless of what you think of your initial dialogue. *Rewrite in progress is usually found to be an excuse for not going on*. Your edit should only happen once you have finished.

And talk out your lines as you write. You may be surprised by what you hear.

PART THREE

Originality is nothing but judicious imitation. The most original writers borrowed from one another. The instruction we find in books is like fire. We fetch it from our neighbors, kindle it at home, communicate it to others, and it becomes the property of all.

Voltaire

THE SCREENPLAY

Here then is *The Prince of Russia* screenplay, which was based on the foregoing twelve page, three-act outline, that was originally on our 12 cards. Now that the action and the setting are well established, note how the dialogue develops each scene and establishes a character-driven story. Their action and the result of that action now become the dramatic content for each and every scene.

I have also included my notes based on the 12-card method to underscore both scene and character development within the screenplay, as our story develops. Furthermore, I have eliminated the typical shot heading, also known as slug lines, for an easier read in my first draft. It changes the format into a novel writing style of storytelling, which I feel is more effective. If the screenplay is optioned for production then the standard shot headings can easily be restored.

* * *

ACT ONE – CARD #1 – (the Set-Up)

FADE IN:

UNDERWATER

as shafts of sunlight refract in all directions. The SOUNDS of breathing through diving regulators are heard as bubbles ascend toward the surface. A DIVER in scuba gear enters the scene and is soon followed by a second DIVER. Below them a FREIGHTER looms out of the fading light. The first diver carefully crosses the silt-covered deck and enters an open HATCH followed by the second diver.

INSIDE THE CARGO HOLD

the first diver leads the way through the obstructions as shafts of SUNLIGHT penetrate the rotting framework. The second diver points to a decomposed CRATE on the cargo floor and swims toward it. The first diver raises his hand in caution as they settle beside the container.

The first diver fans the water above the remains, which removes the silt to expose rows of old disintegrating brass-jacketed 88mm AMMUNITION. The second diver instinctively moves back, flashes a thumbs-up 'okay' to the first diver and they continue to follow the turn of the bilge.

BEGIN OPENING TITLES:

A section of collapsed DECKING angles downward. A jagged HOLE extends up the side of the wreck with rotting beams that sway in the moving SURGE. It looks impassable but the first diver sees a PASSAGEWAY beyond and goes for it.

THE FIRST DIVER

moves through the opening with the second diver close behind. Suddenly the first diver is thrown against the sharp EDGES by the current and snags his neoprene WET SUIT. He struggles to free himself just when the swift outgoing crosscurrent hits, sending him free.

OUTSIDE THE FREIGHTER

the first diver is tossed along the ocean FLOOR with the current. He regains control and turns to face the WRECK, concerned for the other diver's safety.

INSIDE THE FREIGHTER

having seen what happened to the first diver, the other diver carefully calculates the flow of the current then makes his move into the opening. He seems to be in the clear when the reverse current catches him and smashes him against the hull. His REGULATOR is yanked free, he can't reach it and he CAN'T BREATHE!

THE SECOND DIVER

tries frantically to free himself but is held by his tangled AIR HOSE. He tries in vain to reach the HOSE as the SURGE pushes him back and forth. An expression of terror fills his EYES. He can't hold his breath much longer. Suddenly an ARM shoots through the opening as the current reverses and the first diver flips his regulator free and pulls him forward in one desperate move.

THE TWO DIVERS

are swept clear of the wreck by the current to the OUTSIDE. The first diver hands him his regulator and they 'buddy breathe' together until the second diver is able to untangle his regulator to regain his air supply.

OUTSIDE THE FREIGHTER

a sparkling layer of tiny FISH, riding the thermocline, swim through the divers' silvery bubbles as the two divers swim toward the sun-filled SURFACE.

END OF OPENING TITLES

ON THE OCEAN SURFACE

a BOSTON WHALER is tied to a section of the protruding HULL. The divers appear a short distance from the whaler. The second diver rips off his MASK gasping for air and shaken. The first diver swims with him toward the boat.

SUPER: HALIFAX – THE FALL OF 1993

ALONGSIDE THE WHALER

they quickly board at the stern ladder. The second diver appears to struggle on the ladder, still in shock from the experience.

FIRST DIVER
Anatoli! Are you all right?

SECOND DIVER
I'm okay, Mark...
(still recovering)
But that was too close for comfort.

Mark grabs Anatoli's tank and stows it in a nearby rack.

ANATOLI
I really thought I was a goner.

Mark smiles and gives him a friendly slap on the back.

ANATOLI
I owe you one, Mark.

MARK
I'll hold you to that.

Anatoli clears the lines as Mark starts the outboard.

                    ANATOLI
                   (impressed)
          You were pretty cool-headed down there,
          around all those explosives.

The whaler clears the sunken hull and moves out into deeper water. Anatoli removes
his jacket and towels his hair.

                    ANATOLI
          Do you think I worry too much?

                     MARK
          It's part of your Russian nature, I guess.

                    ANATOLI
                  (corrects Mark)
          I'm Estonian, not Russian.

                     MARK
                    (naive)
          There's a difference?

                    ANATOLI
          There's a big difference. We're a sovereign
          nation now, no longer controlled by Russia.

                     MARK
          But you're a Russian officer.

                    ANATOLI
          That may not be for very long.

Mark slams the CONTROLS into forward pushing the throttle all the way. The boat
jumps toward the distant shoreline.

                                        DISSOLVE TO:

SOMETIME LATER ON THE WHALER

Anatoli steps to the helm beside Mark and checks his watch.

ANATOLI
We're going to be right on time for your
father's demo of his new diving suit.

MARK
(uninterested)
I can hardly wait.

DISSOLVE TO:

THE INTERNATIONAL CENTER FOR OCEAN RESEARCH

as the whaler enters the HARBOR. It passes a PIER with a group of research VESSELS
all bearing the ICOR Dolphin Insignia and docks. They secure the lines.

DISSOLVE TO:

INSIDE THE ICOR LOBBY

the large space is lined with a variety of historical photographs of research vessels
and deep-diving equipment from ancient times to the present. The end wall displays a
large photograph of ICOR's latest diving development, a NEWTSUIT. It looks much
like a NASA SPACE SUIT but slightly larger in proportions, with a large acrylic
facemask and special manipulators at the end of the arms.

A RECEPTIONIST

looks up as Mark and Anatoli enter the lobby.

MARK
Good afternoon, Harriet.

HARRIET
(matter-of-fact)
Doctor Fletcher wanted you to suit up for the
demo. I left a message on your service well
over three hours ago.

She picks up a well-traveled LETTER and hands it to Mark.

HARRIET
This letter came for you, but I'd suggest you
read it later. Doctor Fletcher is ready to start!

MARK
(takes the letter)
Thanks, Harriet.

Mark recognizes the postmark, smiles to himself, and stuffs it into his jacket.

DISSOLVE TO:

INSIDE THE LABORATORY TANK ROOM

the space reverberates with the SOUNDS of motors and clanging metal. A CRANE swings across an 80,000 gallon TEST TANK in the middle of the room while a group of TECHNICIANS in white lab coats work at various projects.

ANATOLI

is fascinated by all the activity. They pass a two-man yellow SUBMERSIBLE with a technician fastening a set of high-pressure gas cylinders to the hull. Mark joins him and they pause to watch.

MARK
I used one in Florida last year for a coral
study and it operated perfectly.

Anatoli suddenly glances at his watch.

ANATOLI
(concerned)
I better change into my uniform for the
Demo with the Admiral. I'll see you later.

Mark flashes a mock salute as Anatoli leaves. Then he anxiously rips open his LETTER and his face lights up as he reads the bold handwriting.

DISSOLVE TO:

INSIDE A DARK BOARDROOM AT ICOR

two MEN sit in front of a MONITOR while viewing a TEST that took place in a recompression chamber on an empty NEWTSUIT.

VOICE #1

The Teflon seals on the shoulders of the Newtsuit
are still curling on us. Watch as we reach a depth
beyond two hundred feet.

Suddenly one of the shoulders IMPLODES with a bone crushing SOUND as the seal
quickly disintegrates into the NEWTSUIT, flooding the interior.

VOICE #1

That was at a depth of 235 feet.

VOICE #2

But those seals were designed for operations
beyond 1000 feet or more!

VOICE #1

This is a whole new development for us. It
just isn't right yet, and we're not sure why.

VOICE #2

Have all your tests failed with these seals?

VOICE #1

I'm afraid they have.

VOICE #2

How long to come up with a new seal?

VOICE #1
(unsure)
At least two weeks, maybe longer, it will really
depend on our choice of a new material.

VOICE #2

God damn it Marshall, we don't have that kind
of time and I'm not going to jeopardize all of our
plans just because of this!

MARSHALL

I'm sorry Doctor Fletcher, but I'm afraid
it's very unsafe to operate these Newtsuits
right now, until we solve the problem.

FLETCHER
That's not good enough!

Fletcher steps over to the entranceway and slams on the LIGHTS.

FLETCHER
There's too much at stake. It's your job to fix it.
That's what I pay you for, not for excuses! Give
me one suit at least, for our deep dive tests in
the Baltic with the Russians.

MARSHALL
Give us some extra time onboard. We may be
able to refit one suit for you.

FLETCHER
Then make it your first priority!

The SOUND of Harriet's VOICE is heard over the intercom.

HARRIET (v.o.)
Doctor Fletcher, Admiral Kochinko is ready
for your demonstration.

Fletcher grabs a wall PHONE intercom.

FLETCHER
Tell the Admiral I'm on my way.

He slams the phone down.

FLETCHER
Just remember Marshall, without this contract
with the Russians we're out of business!

MARSHALL
We'll do the best we can, Doctor.

FLETCHER
I want better than that! Now get rid of this
video and don't tell anyone what we've seen
here today, is that understood?

The technician nods in agreement and Fletcher leaves the room.

CUT TO:

INSIDE THE ICOR TANK ROOM

Mark comes to a NEWTSUIT on a stand as a TECHNICIAN attaches a state-of-the-art THRUSTER-PACK to the suit.

> MARK
> Those thrusters look much better than the
> old design.

> TECHNICIAN
> (nods in agreement)
> It's based on your dad's idea.

The technician points to a TERMINAL BOARD on the SUIT.

> TECHNICIAN
> The external mixer board on the suit is still the
> brain for all the maneuvers. The Russian brass
> just loves it!
> (motions towards the tank)
> You can see for yourself.

CUT TO:

MARK'S P.O.V. OF THE DIVER

as he enters the tank in a NEWTSUIT. Nearby a group of RUSSIAN OFFICERS have gathered in front of the viewing WINDOW to watch the diver's descent with his thruster-pack in operation.

CUT TO:

MARK

is unnoticed as he joins the group. Anatoli, now in his UNIFORM, takes his place beside ADMIRAL YURI KOCHINKO who is wearing a white UNIFORM adorned with a variety of military DECORATIONS, and looking very sure of himself.

DOCTOR IAN FLETCHER

enters the scene and takes his place beside the viewing WINDOW.

> **FLETCHER**
> Good afternoon gentlemen. As you may know,
> our Newtsuit is a one atmosphere diving system
> or A.D.S. The best in the world. This suit can put
> a man at 1000 feet, support him for up to twelve
> hours and bring him up immediately without
> decompression and without the bends.

Fletcher turns and cues the DIVER in the tank.

> **FLETCHER**
> Our Diver, Mister Jones, will demonstrate
> our latest thruster-pack program for you.

Now the DIVER, his face visible through an acrylic mask, descends downward with
the thrusters working and lands feet first on the tank bottom. He looks at Fletcher and
gives him a thumbs-up sign as Fletcher activates a MICROPHONE.

> **FLETCHER**
> Carl, select your forward thrusters.

The diver's reply is heard on the overhead SPEAKERS.

> **JONES** (v.o.)
> Roger, Doctor Fletcher.

With astronaut-like dexterity the thrusters move the diver across the tank as he easily
performs a large FIGURE EIGHT over the length of the tank. The Russian OFFICERS
are amazed; especially the old ADMIRAL, and they APPLAUD.

> **ADMIRAL**
> How does he steer himself so well?

> **FLETCHER**
> A foot control system governs left, right,
> forward and aft movements, while a thumb
> switch controls the vertical movement.

ADMIRAL

(impressed)

Very clever, Doctor Fletcher.

FLETCHER

(into the microphone)

Go for the work area, Mister Jones.

Immediately, the multi-jointed NEWTSUIT begins to skip across the floor of the tank to a WORK AREA of pipes and instruments. The diver performs a series of tasks with the claw-like MANIPULATORS, working with tools and equipment.

FLETCHER

Be aware that the diver can jettison his
thruster pack at any time.

Carl responds and disengages the THRUSTER PACK with ease.

FLETCHER

We can also jettison the umbilical cord and
the diver can sustain on two closed circuits
O-2 life support systems for twelve hours.

Carl jettisons his UMBILICAL system and looks out at Fletcher.

FLETCHER

Now for the encore, Mister Jones!

Carl lays face down, and then slowly elevates himself into a HANDSTAND while balancing on his two manipulators. A Russian PHOTOGRAPHER steps forward and takes a series of pictures. Carl smiles back at him while holding his handstand, then tumbles back onto his feet. The enthusiastic Russian OFFICERS give him a loud round of APPLAUSE. Carl smiles again and takes a short bow.

ADMIRAL

(approaches Fletcher)

Well, I'm certainly looking forward to our
diving trials with you, Doctor Fletcher. Your
Newtsuit performance is very impressive but
how will it operate in a five knot Baltic current?

FLETCHER
You'll be pleasantly surprised, Admiral.

Fletcher now notices Mark standing nearby and responds with a wave.

FLETCHER
Mark, I didn't see you there.

MARK
I just arrived about ten minutes ago.

FLETCHER
I was hoping you'd be here earlier.

Mark disregards the remark as Fletcher makes the introduction.

FLETCHER
My son Mark. This is Admiral Yuri Kochinko,
who is head of acquisitions for the Kakhimov
Naval Academy at Kronstadt.

MARK
Nice to meet you, Admiral.

ADMIRAL
(shaking hands)
It is my pleasure.

FLETCHER
I was hoping that Mark would demonstrate
the Newtsuit for us this afternoon, but I guess
he had more important things to do.

MARK
I'm sorry; I didn't get your message earlier.
We were offshore diving on the Langley Ridge,
an old freighter that went down in 1935.

The Admiral senses the tension between them.

ADMIRAL

Don't be too hard on him, Doctor. We soon
forget the challenges of youth when it comes
to the sea, you should know that.
(smiles at Mark)
Have you been to Russia before?

MARK

Yes, I have. We visited my grandfather
there when I was sixteen. My mother was
born in Tallinn.

Mark hesitates for a moment, that particular image creates a sad expression on his
face. The Admiral turns to Fletcher, looking surprised.

ADMIRAL

You never mentioned you had a Russian
wife, Doctor Fletcher.

FLETCHER

She died about six years ago.

The Admiral's jovial mood quickly changes.

ADMIRAL

I'm so sorry to hear that.

The Admiral turns back to Mark trying to repair his faux pas.

ADMIRAL

Do you speak Russian?

MARK

I only remember a few words.

A Russian Officer approaches the Admiral and salutes smartly.

OFFICER

Excuse me Admiral, the photographer
is ready for us, sir.

ADMIRAL
Excellent. I'll be right there.
(turns to Fletcher and Mark)
I'll see you both on the flight.

FLETCHER
I'm looking forward to that.

They shake hands and the Admiral leaves.

CUT TO:

* * *

That is the end of CARD #1, which is approximately ten minutes of screen time. And we end with a 'cliff-hanger' now that we know that the shoulder seals on the Newtsuit are flawed and may not be repaired in time for the diving trials, along with Fletcher depending on the Russian contract to save his company.

*You may also note that we opened our story with a life-or-death underwater scene, known in Hollywood as "a car chase." These brief underwater **images** establish the mood and a strong sense of where we are for our audience. And with these images we create a **metaphor** for our film; the harsh, unforgiving environment of the sea and a man's struggle to survive.*

This opening also establishes Mark as a cool professional who knows his way around an underwater world. It is important to establish that fact with our audience, at the very beginning of our story, to make his future activities plausible. Mark even saves the life of his Estonian visitor. Now we need to explore Mark's relationship with his father, and what the future holds for them.

* * *

ACT ONE – CARD #2

Mark and his father step to one side, away from the activity.

MARK
We need to have a talk.

FLETCHER
Make it fast, I'm behind schedule.

MARK

I won't be with you on this trip. Once we get to
St. Petersburg I'm going on to stay with Nikolai.

FLETCHER

When did all this happen?

MARK

Nick is onto something. I just got another letter
and he wants me to join him on a special dive.

FLETCHER
(not impressed)
Another treasure hunt?

Fletcher is both surprised and disappointed by Mark's decision.

MARK

This one is different. They've really found
something called, The Prince of Russia.

FLETCHER

What'n the hell is that?

MARK

It was a Russian freighter that was lost at the
end of the war carrying a U.S. gold shipment
to Leningrad and he wants me on the dive.

FLETCHER

That was over fifty years ago. Someone has
already salvaged the gold by now.

MARK

It took them two months to locate her and I
really want to help Nikolai on this dive.

FLETCHER

So why didn't you ask my opinion first?

MARK

I figured it was my decision to make.

FLETCHER

What about me? I have to replace you right
away. I was counting on your help on this trip.

MARK

Nick needs my help and I need to get away on
my own. Take Carl with you, he's just as good.

FLETCHER

Mark, I don't need to hear this. I've got too
many problems to work out before we leave.

Fletcher turns to leave, then steps back, face to face in a low voice.

FLETCHER

This sale with the Russians could make or
break this company, and you should know
that. If you don't want to be part of my team
that's your decision, but you're only hurting
yourself.

Before Mark can reply a technician enters the scene.

TECHNICIAN

Excuse me, Doctor... we're all set for you.

FLETCHER

I'm coming right now.

Fletcher leaves Mark standing alone, frustrated and angry.

DISSOLVE TO:

AN AEROFLOT JUMBO JET (stock)

appears almost motionless in the SKY as far below a flat strata-field of orange clouds
captures the early morning SUNRISE.

DISSOLVE TO:

ON A CHESSBOARD

a HAND moves in ready to pick up a white knight, then pauses for the moment.

MARK (v.o.)
That's not a good idea...

The hand quickly CASTLES the WHITE KING into hiding.

CAMERA WIDENS:

MARK AND ANATOLI

are seated together, beside a window, with a CHESSBOARD between them.

ANATOLI
That's a good choice...

CAMERA MOVES TO:

FLETCHER AND THE ADMIRAL

are seated diagonally across the aisle from Mark, with a tray of DRINKS.

ADMIRAL
We have planned four days of preparation
then we leave on the Nordenskiøld. She is
one of our most advanced research vessels.

FLETCHER
How many days of diving?

ADMIRAL
We'll conduct six days of tests in the Baltic
with the Newtsuit, then return to Kronstadt
for all of our dry tests in the lab. Does that
sound reasonable to you?

The Admiral takes a long drink of his Vodka and waits for Fletcher's comment. Fletcher appears uneasy with the plan but covers his concern with a positive nod.

FLETCHER
Yes, it does Admiral. However, I may need
some time for adjustments on our Newtsuit
before we make our deep dives in the Baltic.

ADMIRAL
I understand.

The Admiral snaps his fingers and the Russian CAMERAMAN suddenly appears. He raises his glass of Vodka for a toast to Fletcher.

ADMIRAL
To our future success. Skøl!

The camera flashes. The Admiral drains his glass. Fletcher follows with some difficulty. The camera flashes again. The Admiral is pleased with himself and pours another round.

ADMIRAL
I heard that your son won't be with you on
these dives, after all.

FLETCHER
That's correct. Mark has decided to spend
some time with his grandfather in Tallinn.

ADMIRAL
It's one of my favorite towns.

FLETCHER
I was hoping he would want to join our
dive team.

ADMIRAL
Lieutenant Tsarkov told me that Mark saved
his life yesterday, while they were diving.

FLETCHER
(surprised)
He never told me about that.

ADMIRAL
(changes the subject)
What does your father-in-law do in Tallinn?

FLETCHER
He was a salvage diver with the Baltic Fleet.

                    ADMIRAL
          That can be a very interesting profession.
          Has he found anything of value?

                    FLETCHER
          Mark tells me that he's located an old freighter
          that was carrying an American gold shipment
          to Russia, during the war.

The Admiral's expression quickly changes.

                    ADMIRAL
          A gold shipment?

                    FLETCHER
          Supposedly... Mark said it went down toward
          the end of the war.

                    ADMIRAL
          Do they know the name of the ship?

                    FLETCHER
          His grandfather said it was, The Prince of
          Russia. Have you heard of it?

He looks over at Fletcher and forces a brief, nervous expression.

                    ADMIRAL
                  (dead pans)
          No... I don't think so. There were many
          Russian freighters in service, at that time.

The Admiral drains his glass and stares out the window, looking uncomfortable.

                                        SLOW DISSOLVE:

SOMETIME LATER (STOCK)

the airliner begins to descend through a light layer of clouds to reveal the BALTIC
SEA in all its glory, far below. It is a breathtaking scene.

INSIDE THE AIRLINER

Mark and Anatoli have just finished another game of chess.

> MARK
> That's four even.

> ANATOLI
> You're not a bad player for a Canadian.

> MARK
> You're not exactly a Boris Spassky yourself.

The SOUND of a landing announcement is heard in Russian, and then repeated in English as the jet continues to slowly descend. Mark glances out the window.

> CUT TO:

MARK'S P.O.V. OF THE BAY OF FINLAND

as the afternoon SUN sparkles across the distant azure Baltic sea.

> ANATOLI (v.o.)
> You might be able to see the Kronstadt Naval
> Yard from here as we approach St. Petersburg.

> CUT TO:

MARK

sits back with a satisfied look on his face.

> MARK
> This time tomorrow I'll be on a train to Tallinn.

> ANATOLI
> You'll enjoy it. It's about a ten-hour trip.

> MARK
> That's all right... I can't wait to start on the
> dive with Nikolai.

ANATOLI

You're lucky; it really sounds like a great
adventure for you.

MARK

Why don't you come with us?

ANATOLI

Wish I could... but the Admiral tells me that
I'll be in charge of lab tests with the back-up
Newtsuit while your father is off diving.

Anatoli looks up and smiles, covering his disappointment.

ANATOLI

Anyway, the weather's great, the sun hardly
sets in June. You'll have a great time.

The Russian PHOTOGRAPHER suddenly appears with his camera.

PHOTOGRAPHER

The Admiral wants a picture. Is that okay?

Anatoli puts his arm around Mark and strikes a heroic pose with a broad smile. The
camera is focused. A sudden flash and the picture is taken.

DISSOLVE TO:

THE INTERNATIONAL AIRPORT IN ST. PETERSBURG

as Mark and Anatoli arrive with their bags. Suddenly a lovely young WOMAN rushes
through the crowd toward Anatoli.

THE WOMAN

Anatoli, you're back! (Estonian)

She immediately embraces him with kisses on both cheeks.

ANATOLI

Kalin... how good to see you. (Estonian)

Anatoli swings her off her feet with delight. Mark is slightly embarrassed by such a familiar encounter. Anatoli looks over at Mark and winks with a bright smile.

ANATOLI
One of my many admirers.

She pushes him away; faces Mark and speaks perfect English.

THE WOMAN
You must be Mark Fletcher.

MARK
Yes, I am...

THE WOMAN
Anatoli tells me that you're the Jacques
Cousteau of the Atlantic coastline.

Mark looks over at Anatoli and shakes his head in disbelief.

ANATOLI
(playful)
You can see that such secret information
travels fast in our country.

THE WOMAN
(offers her hand)
I'm Kalin... Anatoli's cousin and I'm very
glad to meet you. Welcome to our country.

Mark is obviously impressed by this lovely, energetic lady.

MARK
Thank you...

ANATOLI
Mark is going on to Tallinn, to visit his
grandfather.

KALIN
(surprised)
Really, that's where I live. My mother
and I have a bookstore there.

Mark looks over at Anatoli, unsure of what else to say to Kalin.

MARK
You didn't tell me you had a beautiful
cousin.

ANATOLI
(grins)
You didn't ask me.

Mark looks at Kalin and they exchange a pleasant smile. Mark is smitten. Anatoli and
Mark pick up their bags and Kalin leads them towards the airport exit.

DISSOLVE TO:

OUTSIDE ADMIRAL KOCHINKO'S RESIDENCE

that evening in ST. PETERSBURG, a black VOLVO enters the DRIVEWAY and comes
to a stop. The athletic figure of a man in a MILITARY uniform appears and sprints
toward the entrance. He inserts a pass number on the pad and enters.

INSIDE ADMIRAL KOCHINKO'S STUDY

the Admiral appears agitated as he chews on an unlit cigar behind a large elegant
DESK. The oak-paneled walls are covered with photographs of military accomplish-
ments, awards and citations to a distinguished Naval career.

Sitting opposite the General, in a leather armchair, is a portly man, VIKTOR
ALFERENKO. He is neatly dressed in a custom made suit and wears dark glasses.

VIKTOR
What makes you think they can involve us?

The Admiral nervously stubs his unlit cigar into an ashtray before he answers.

ADMIRAL

Because when this old diver climbs onboard
The Prince of Russia, the whole investigation
will start all over again, that's why. Damn him!

VIKTOR

It's been forty-eight years. That old freighter
has to be a pile of junk by now.

ADMIRAL

That doesn't matter. I don't want anyone
onboard, ever again. We don't need this!

VIKTOR

Yuri, there's no real evidence. You're being
paranoid. We're the only living survivors
and we've destroyed all the records.

ADMIRAL

When they find that freighter we stand to lose
everything and all because of this old man!

Viktor reaches over and takes a cigar from the Admiral's silver HUMIDOR on the
desk. He casually lights it, before suggesting his solution.

VIKTOR
(matter-of-fact)
I can arrange to have his finances frozen at
his bank and bankrupt him. That'll put him
out of business. No equipment, no diving.

That's not what the Admiral had in mind, but he likes that idea..

ADMIRAL

That's excellent. You can organize that. But
what we really need is to destroy his ability
to succeed. I'll show you what I have in mind.

The Admiral anxiously punches a key on his desk INTERCOM.

ADMIRAL
Has the Lieutenant arrived?

SECRETARY (v.o.)
Yes Admiral, he has.

ADMIRAL
Good, send him in.

SECRETARY (v.o.)
Right away sir.

A rugged-looking soldier in his twenties enters wearing a Special Forces uniform with a distinctive red beret. He is the man we saw arriving in the black Volvo. The Lieutenant comes to attention at the desk and salutes the Admiral smartly.

OFFICER
Lieutenant Boris Gorzenko, reporting sir!

ADMIRAL
Lieutenant Gorzenko, I'd like you to meet
a friend of mine, Commissar Viktor Alferenko.
Viktor is the Economic Chairman of the
Promstroibank, here in St. Petersburg.

Gorzenko steps forward and they shake hands.

GORZENKO
Nice to meet you, sir.

ADMIRAL
The Lieutenant is with Special Forces.

The Admiral hands Gorzenko a manila envelope marked CONFIDENTIAL.

ADMIRAL
We had a talk earlier today and the
Lieutenant is well aware of the urgency
of his assignment. And I believe we both
understand each other?

GORZENKO
(nods)
Yes, Admiral, we certainly do.

Viktor nods in agreement, he looks pleased with this plan.

ADMIRAL
Good hunting, Lieutenant.

GORZENKO
Thank you, sir. We'll be in touch.

Gorzenko nods to Viktor, then smartly turns and strides toward the door.

DISSOLVE TO:

THE NEXT AFTERNOON A LOCOMOTIVE (STOCK)

rattles along the COAST winding through seaside settlements. The sun appears from behind dark rain-clouds, washing the horizon out to SEA in a golden glow.
Over this scene we hear the SOUNDS of Eric Clapton and the Jailbirds ...

DISSOLVE TO:

INSIDE A COACH

that is half empty, Mark is sprawled out with an English/Russian DICTIONARY wearing a set of EARPHONES, the source of the Rock Music. A light rain streaks down the window beside him. A moment later, Mark closes the dictionary and decides to look out the window at the passing countryside.

CUT TO:

MARK'S P.O.V. OF THE COUNTRYSIDE (STOCK)

as haystacks, iron red cattle and fields of clover rush by. The wet, rich earth is a dark chocolate with fields of golden grain and orchards.

CUT TO:

MARK

turns back to the dictionary and continues studying. He is determined to learn as much as he can, but his thoughts are elsewhere. Finally he puts the dictionary aside to enjoy the music, feeling homesick for the moment, as the train moves on.

CUT TO:

THE LOCOMOTIVE (STOCK)

continues into the TWILIGHT passing seaside cafes, narrow beaches and rural settlements along the limestone coastline, marked by numerous bays and inlets.

SLOW FADE TO:

THE FOLLOWING MORNING

Mark is asleep as the CONDUCTOR enters the coach and announces the next stop in a loud VOICE as the train slows down.

CONDUCTOR
Tallin, Tallin station is our next stop!

Mark wakes up and stumbles out into the aisle still half-asleep. He pulls down his luggage from the overhead rack.

IN THE TALLINN RAILROAD STATION

An athletic looking MAN in a colorful embroidered SHIRT steps onto the busy PLATFORM searching the CROWD for a familiar face.

MARK

steps out of the COACH with his luggage and looks around.

CUT TO:

A PHOTOGRAPH OF MARK AND ANATOLI

is being held in a black gloved HAND. It is a photograph that the Admiral's photographer had taken on the airplane. The fingers neatly fold the photograph in half revealing only the face of MARK.

CAMERA WIDENS TO:

BORIS GORZENKO

dressed in street clothes, slips the photograph into his jacket and walks along the platform. He suddenly recognizes Mark in the crowd and moves toward him.

MARK

is still checking the CROWD for a familiar face. Suddenly, the man in the embroidered shirt comes out of the crowd and throws a bear hug on Mark.

                        THE MAN
                    Mark Fletcher!

                          MARK
                    Sergei, you old bear!

BORIS GORZENKO

watches the two men for a moment, then he leaves the platform.

MARK AND SERGEI

are delighted to see each other.

                          MARK
                    Sergei, I can't believe it's you, full beard
                    and all. You look great.

Sergei helps Mark with his luggage.

                        SERGEI
                    Let's get to my truck and get out of here.

IN THE STATION PARKING LOT

the enormous glass dome of the station catches the morning sun. Sergei's old 1969 Mercedes TRUCK soon appears and drives out of the parking lot.

GORZENKO

is sitting nearby behind the wheel of his black VOLVO, parked on the street. When Sergei's truck appears, Gorzenko quickly follows at a safe distance.

                                                        CUT TO:

                            *   *   *

*These scenes further establish Fletcher as a taskmaster and what he expects from others around him, especially his son. However, Mark is at an age for the need to find his own way, right or wrong. This becomes our **inciting incident**. It establishes the problems between Mark and his father and creates the motivation for Mark to go forward in his quest with his grandfather. He may be facing a grave danger but he wants to face that risk in his life, on his own terms.*

*Little do they suspect that their relationship with Admiral Kochinko will change their lives forever. Maybe our audience already senses this; they certainly know that Gorzenko is up to no good. This alone introduces a second **turning point** and quickly establishes a **ticking clock** for most of our audience to dwell on. This happens right at the beginning of our story, and only the audience knows.*

*   *   *

ACT ONE – CARD #3

INSIDE THE TRUCK CAB

Mark's attention is drawn to a series of steep limestone RAMPARTS beside the road. Sergei points at an ancient FORT, just beyond the ramparts.

> SERGEI
> Do you remember that place?

> MARK
> (nods)
> There's a castle up there.

CUT TO:

MARK'S P.O.V. OF THE TOWN

as the sunrise highlights the ramparts of the UPPER TOWN swathed in greenery. The tall STEEPLES of medieval towers and copper-covered church SPIRES sparkle from the recent rainfall.

> MARK (v.o.)
> We were there eight years ago. I raced you to
> the top of the tower and won twenty-rubles
> with my bet that I could beat you.

INSIDE THE TRUCK CAB

they both laugh at the image. Sergei turns toward Mark.

> SERGEI
> That's only because a guard stopped me first.
> He didn't notice you because you were so skinny.

> MARK
> I bet I could beat you again!

> SERGEI
> (smiles)
> You probably could.

DISSOLVE TO:

THE COASTAL HIGHWAY

as the TRUCK moves into the distance followed by the VOLVO.

DISSOLVE TO:

A SIGN BESIDE THE SALVAGE YARD GATEWAY READS:

> NIKOLAI GORGASALI
> Marine Salvage & Diesel Repair

CAMERA WIDENS:

SERGEI'S TRUCK

enters the gate, passes a DRY-DOCK and an aging WORKBOAT. The truck stops beside an old canal BARGE that appears to be newly renovated.

CUT TO:

MARK'S P.O.V. OF THE BARGE

The cargo area has been converted to a spacious living quarters with a timbered building and a tiled roof. Smoke drifts from a chimney. Docked just in front of the barge is a 200-ton refitted SALVAGE TUG in the process of being RE-PAINTED.

CUT TO:

MARK

quickly crosses the GANGPLANK onto the BARGE, as Sergei goes to the tug. Mark pauses for a moment by the entrance to the GALLEY to look around. The SOUND of ESTONIAN MUSIC is heard coming from one of the open WINDOWS.

THE BLACK VOLVO

has come to a stop just outside the GATE. Gorzenko appears and cautiously steps inside the gate and carefully surveys the area through a pair of BINOCULARS.

CUT TO:

GORZENKO'S P.O.V. THROUGH THE BINOCULARS

as he PANS along the barge, past the gangplank, to the bow of the tug and comes to rest on the name: THE BALTIC STAR, painted in large white letters.

CUT TO:

GORZENKO

returns to his car and writes in a NOTEBOOK. He then picks up a TELEPHONE and makes a call, all the while watching for any activity in the dry-dock.

INSIDE THE BARGE GALLEY

NIKOLAI expertly chops a head of cabbage on a wooden block while humming to the music from a nearby radio. He is an energetic man with a full head of gray hair and a broad mustache. A steaming Kapooska soup in an iron pot sits on an old wood-burning STOVE. Mark enters the galley just as Nikolai looks up.

NIKOLAI
I'm so glad you're here, safe and sound.

MARK
After reading your last letter, I figured
you'd need an extra hand on this dive.

Nikolai drops the chopped cabbage into the soup pot with a flourish.

NIKOLAI

Well you're just in time to have my fish
Zapekanaka. I made it in your honor.

He opens an OVEN and checks on a FISH CASSEROLE with a fork.

NIKOLAI

How's your father?

MARK

He's fine... I guess.

NIKOLAI

He sounds very unhappy that you're not
with him on these dive tests.

MARK
(surprised to hear this)
When did you talk to him?

Nikolai stirs a batter of egg yolks and herbs into the soup.

NIKOLAI
(matter-of-fact)
He called last night and we talked. I gave
him a few good tips on how he should sell
his Newtsuit to the Russians.

Sergei now bursts into the galley, changing the mood.

SERGEI
(to Mark)
Your cabin onboard the tug is ship-shape,
with your luggage stowed under the bunk.
Do you have any questions?

MARK

Yes, an important one. When do we sail?

NIKOLAI

Sooner than you think.

SOMETIME LATER IN THE DINING ROOM

a long TABLE has the remains of the meal. Nikolai adjusts a pair of reading GLASSES, and then looks over at Sergei and WINKS.

NIKOLAI
Let's show Mark where the gold is.

Sergei looks over at Mark with a suspicious scowl on his face.

SERGEI
How do you know we can trust him?

They both laugh. Mark only shakes his head at their bad performance. Nikolai goes to a SIDEBOARD and rolls out a MARINE CHART of the BALTIC SEA onto the table. He adjusts his glasses, and points to the dive site.

CUT TO:

MARK'S P.O.V. OF THE MARINE CHART

shows the north-east sector off the coast of Estonia. Nikolai taps on a tiny island.

NIKOLAI (v.o.)
The dive site is a one-hour trip to the south
west of the island of Hiiumaa.

CUT TO:

AT THE TABLE

Nikolai points to an oceanic layered dark blue RIDGE just off the coastline.

NIKOLAI
Sitting on this narrow ridge at a depth of 240
feet sits The Prince of Russia. It's a 5000-ton
Russian freighter that went down in 1945 with
a large American gold shipment. It was on its
way to Leningrad to help the Russian war effort.
(looks over at Mark)

We calculate it's carrying some forty million
in gold ingots that are still onboard.

Mark's eyes widen at the vision of that much gold.

MARK
You've actually seen this freighter?

NIKOLAI
It took two months to locate her.

SERGEI
Nick made his first dive three weeks ago,
just after we found her.

NIKOLAI
It has settled keel down on a narrow ridge,
but it's all in one piece.

MARK
That sounds really fantastic.

SERGEI
Nik even read the name on the stern. Wanted
to board, but it became impossible because of
a bad sow'easter that suddenly blew up.

NIKOLAI
We had to quickly pull anchor and make a run
for it. But with you here it's there for the taking!

Nikolai goes back to the sideboard and holds up a traditional ELK DRINKING HORN.
It is ornately carved with pastoral scenes and neatly trimmed in silver.

NIKOLAI
Now the most important part of our evening.
This is a tanzi, an Estonian drinking horn.
My father made when he was your age.
(steps back to the table)
It has been waiting all these years to join
us here tonight for our celebration.

Nikolai carefully empties almost a bottle of Tsinandali WINE into the upright horn. Then he holds it up and proposes the first TOAST.

NIKOLAI
May the good Lord keep us in His hand
and never close His fist too tight.

Nikolai takes a long drink, then hands it to Sergei to make a toast.

SERGEI
(winks at Nik)
May we live to be a hundred years,
with one extra year to repent.

He takes a longer drink and hands it ceremoniously to Mark with a sly smile.

MARK
To our health and our good fortune.

Mark tilts the horn for a drink, which allows the remaining trapped wine to be released all over him. He looks suspiciously at the horn. They burst out laughing.

MARK
(feeling foolish)
I just figured this out.

He looks up and wipes his face. Nikolai refills the horn and hands it to Mark.

NIKOLAI
Now it's your turn to start.

Mark is careful to take a long drink, then he hands it to Sergei.

DISSOLVE TO:

INSIDE THE ENGINE ROOM OF THE BALTIC STAR

GORZENKO is hooded and dressed in black fatigues. He steps out of the shadows with a flashlight to examine the ENGINE. He shines his light at the lower cavity of the bilge looking for a specific piece of equipment under the big diesel.

CUT TO:

GORZENKO'S P.O.V. OF THE MAIN SEACOCK

as his flashlight illuminates the large VALVE that is securely connected to the framework of the hull with five sturdy BOLTS.

CUT TO:

GORZENKO

drops down on his stomach and slides forward toward the valve for a closer look.

DISSOLVE TO:

SOMETIME LATER MARK AND NIKOLAI

stagger up the gangplank to the BALTIC STAR. Both are feeling the effects of the wine as they step unsteadily onto the deck. They cross to the railing to look out at the shimmering BALTIC SEA. A full MOON commands the clear night sky.

> NIKOLAI
> This is my favorite time of the year.
> (sniffs the air)
> Can you smell that?

> MARK
> Mmm... what is it?

> NIKOLAI
> The fishermen are burning alder wood
> to cure their herring catch of the day.

THE COMPANIONWAY TO THE ENGINE ROOM

as Gorzenko appears and watches them for a moment. Then he moves toward the gangplank, but Nikolai sees him and tries to stop him by stepping in his way.

> NIKOLAI
> What're you doin' onboard?

Gorzenko knocks Nikolai aside. Mark tries to stop him but an arm like a coiled spring chops him on the neck and he is sent reeling. Nikolai gets to his feet, but Gorzenko is already down the gangplank and quickly disappears into the night.

MARK
What was all that about?

NIKOLAI
I don't know, but we better keep an eye
open from now on.

LATER THAT EVENING IN MARK'S CABIN

he removes a framed PHOTOGRAPH while unpacking his luggage.

CUT TO:

MARK'S P.O.V. OF THE PHOTO IN A GOLD FRAME

of his mother. A sixteen-year old Mark is with her on a sailboat. They are smiling
with their arms around each other at this happy family event.

CUT TO:

MARK

sets the photograph down, climbs into the bunk, and turns out the light. Moonlight
fills the open porthole, just above his head. He can hear the hush of waves against the
harbor wall as he closes his eyes and falls asleep.

SLOW DISSOLVE TO:

ONBOARD THE BARGE

Nikolai is at a CHART-TABLE in his STUDY smoking his pipe. The walls are covered
in nautical photographs and sketches of ships. His TELEPHONE rings.

NIKOLAI
Allo.

FLETCHER (v.o.)
Nikolai, it's Ian. I'm calling from the Kronstadt.
Is Mark still up?

NIKOLAI
I think he's asleep, but I can wake him.

FLETCHER ONBOARD THE R. V. NORDENSKIØLD

is walking along the deck talking into a ship-to-shore TELEPHONE.

> FLETCHER
> No, don't disturb him. He's most likely
> sleeping off the jet-lag.

All around him supplies and equipment are being loaded onboard. A battery of powerful dock LIGHTS illuminate the vessel and the two gangplanks.

> FLETCHER
> We're still setting up our diving system.
> We hope to leave in four days.

Fletcher continues walking towards the stern.

> FLETCHER
> We're on schedule, just some adjustments
> that have to be made on our Newtsuit.

He comes to a RAILING that overlooks the STERN DECK.

CUT TO:

FLETCHER'S P.O.V. OF RUSSIAN TECHNICIANS

that are gathered around a NEWTSUIT on a stand with CARL JONES. He is explaining the special diving functions on a chalkboard.

> FLETCHER (v.o.)
> No... these can't corrode in salt-water. Teflon
> and titanium high-pressure seals. They're the
> the most reliable under all conditions.

CUT TO:

FLETCHER

now turns and climbs a staircase to the UPPER DECK

> FLETCHER.
> No, Nik... they're not the kind of seals that
> you have in your old hard-hat equipment.
> (he laughs)
> For God's sake, Nik, your stuff is over thirty
> years old! I wouldn't trust it.

The SOUND of a HELICOPTER is heard approaching the ship.

> FLETCHER
> How're you doing with your bank loan
> for The Baltic Star?

Fletcher checks his WATCH, then looks up into the night sky.

> FLETCHER
> Nik... if I had the money I'd give it to you.
> When will you know about the loan?

CUT TO:

NIKOLAI AT THE CHART-TABLE

taps out the ashes from his pipe into an ashtray and begins a refill.

> NIKOLAI
> We'll know tomorrow. An officer is coming
> from the Promstroibank. I'm sure they'll
> extend my credit, after all I served with the
> Baltic Fleet for twenty-years. That should
> mean something to the bankers.
> (lights up)
> Alright, Ian... I'll tell Mark you called. Take
> care of yourself. _Dobry vyecher_.

Nikolai hangs up the phone looking tired and a little concerned.

CUT TO:

A SIKORSKY SEA-KING HELICOPTER

touches down on the ship's LANDING PAD. A moment later, the ADMIRAL climbs down a short step and walks clear of the draft from the swirling BLADES overhead. Fletcher meets him and they shake hands.

> FLETCHER (v.o.)
> Welcome aboard, Admiral. How was your flight?

Fletcher and the Admiral head towards the stern STAIRCASE.

> ADMIRAL (v.o.)
> (indifferent)
> I could use a drink right now!

AT THE RAILING THAT OVERLOOKS THE STERN DECK

the Admiral appears to be very impressed with all of the activity.

> ADMIRAL
> How is your son doing on his treasure dive?

> FLETCHER
> (caught off guard)
> Mark?

> ADMIRAL
> Yes, Mark. When does The Baltic Star set sail?

Fletcher is surprised that the Admiral knows the name of Nikolai's tug. He can't remember ever mentioning the name.

> FLETCHER
> I'm not sure...
> (looks at him)
> How'd you know the name of Nik's tugboat?

> ADMIRAL
> (matter-of-fact)
> You told me on the flight.

FLETCHER
(can't recall)
I did?

The old Admiral looks over at him and nods confidently.

ADMIRAL
Let's go below. We can both use a drink.

SLOW DISSOLVE TO:

SUNRISE THE FOLLOWING MORNING

as gulls and terns soar along the BAY OF TALLINN. A gentle swell surges against the outer breakwater that protects the inner harbor from the approaching SEA.

INSIDE MARK'S CABIN

he is still sleeping. Suddenly his tranquility is shattered by the explosive SOUNDS of RIVETS hitting the deck plates overhead. Mark bolts upright, smashing his head against an overhead pipe, as the deafening sound continues.

CUT TO:

SERGEI WITH A RIVET-GUN

is busy resetting RIVETS in the DECK. Nikolai is measuring CABLE and smoking his pipe. Mark stumbles onto the deck rubbing his sore head, still half-asleep.

SERGEI
(to Mark)
You've got a hangover from the wine?

Mark shakes his head, remembering his assailant from last night.

MARK
No, it's not that. Someone was onboard last
night, nailed me with a fist and took off.

SERGEI
Nik was telling me, so I had a look around
this morning to see if there's anything missing.

MARK

Maybe he was looking for a place to sleep.

SERGEI

I doubt that. He was likely trying to steal
some equipment, until you came onboard.

Nikolai goes back to measuring cable.

NIKOLAI

There's breakfast in the galley and when
you get back I have a perfect job for you.

SLOW FADE TO:

SOMETIME LATER

Mark is swinging from a BOSON'S CHAIR just above the waterline. He has a bucket
and a brush and is carefully painting the trim around a porthole.

AN OLD LADA CAR

stops near the tug's gangplank. A man carrying a briefcase boards the tug and is met
by Nikolai and they shake hands. Nikolai then steps over to the railing and looks down
at Mark suspended on the boson's chair.

NIKOLAI

Mark, come up and join us.

INSIDE THE DINING ROOM

the man searches through his disorganized briefcase.

NIKOLAI

Mark, this is Mister Tulchinsky from the
Promstroibank.

MARK

Good morning.

Tulchinsky nods as he continues searching his briefcase. He finds an ENVELOPE and
hands it to Nikolai. He opens it, squints at the page, then passes it to Sergei.

NIKOLAI
You should read this, Sergei. I don't have my
glasses with me.

SERGEI
Dear Comrade Gorgasali. As you know the
Industrial and Construction Bank is responsible
for financing large industrial building projects
and for providing credits to industry such as your
marine-salvage enterprise.

Sergei pauses to look over at Nikolai.

NIKOLAI
(anxious)
Go on... keep reading.

SERGEI
In the past many enterprises used credit
facilities to cover their long term financial
shortfalls and losses due to their economic
mismanagement

Nikolai just shakes his head, he already knows the answer.

SERGEI
Our Board of Directors have decided that the
use of such ongoing credit for these purposes
will not be allowed in the future...

Sergei pauses nervously to clear his throat before continuing.

SERGEI
Unfortunately, since you are a loss-making
enterprise, we cannot extend your credit at this
time to cover the final payments on The Baltic
Star. Yours sincerely, Viktor Alferenko
Economic Chairman.

Nikolai grabs the letter from Sergei and waves it at Tulchinsky.

NIKOLAI
(angry)
I can't understand this. All of a sudden they've
now changed their minds. The last time we met
I was assured of the loan! What happened
between then and now?

TULCHINSKY
(matter-of-fact)
I'm sorry; it's out of my hands.

SERGEI
We're not asking for a lot of money.

TULCHINSKY
(ignores Sergei)
The bank has decided to liquidate your assets,
including your dry dock facilities, to cover your
outstanding debts.

NIKOLAI
And when do you plan to do that?

TULCHINSKY
Commissar Alferenko will allow you seventy-
two hours to meet his demands, then we will
seize your assets.

Nikolai jumps to his feet and comes around the table to confront him.

NIKOLAI
That's impossible. We can't raise that kind of
money in three days. The bank knows that!

Tulchinsky calmly closes his briefcase and stands.

TULCHINSKY
I'm sorry, it is not my decision. If there are
no further questions I will be leaving.

SERGEI
We have no further questions.

Tulchinsky leaves. There is a moment of silence among the three men, then Nikolai angrily smashes his fist down on the table.

NIKOLAI
It's not over yet!

SERGEI
We need to dive as soon as possible.

NIKOLAI
It means we should leave for the dive site
within twenty-four hours. Can we do that?

SERGEI
That's cutting our prep time very short, but
we can do it. Once we're out at sea it's going
to be tough for them to stop us.

MARK
(determined)
I agree with Sergei. Let's go for it!

They both look over at Mark. Nikolai has to smile at his enthusiasm.

DISSOLVE TO:

* * *

That is the end of Act One and it has introduced all of our main characters in the story. I believe that there is nothing more satisfying to an audience, at this point in our storytelling, then to actually have our villain, or villains, come face to face with our heroes, in the beginning of the first act. In this case, it was a brief encounter but it still foretells to our audience what our trio will be facing.

*This unexpected situation for Nikolai with the bank deciding to seize his assets within seventy-two hours happens around page 20 to 25 in the screenplay which creates our first major **plot point**. Our main characters are determined to have a successful dive for the gold, and be happy ever after. But we have now introduced an element that could easily change all of that. Unbeknown to them, Gorzenko and the Admiral are just as determined to stop them at any price; a life or death scenario emerges. Our story will now be taken in a new direction. A progression of small events in the First Act has brought us to this change of direction. Now our characters must face* *a series of difficult obstacles to reach their goal, especially Mark. This should also produce more **empathy** from our audience as they identify with such difficulties.*

*As we are about to enter the Second Act, I have noticed that the flaws in most films seem to take place in this act. This is the act that holds your beginning and end together and you should know exactly how to handle that precarious bond. It's an opportunity to dig deep and explore all of your characters, reveal their shortcomings and their fears. The tough part is staying on course in the second act, building your story, making it impossible for your protagonist or your antagonist to succeed. Keep in mind that most important ingredient: **conflict**.*

*Conflict creates drama. Without conflict your storytelling will lack momentum and come to a dismal stop, well before the resolution takes place. Continue to raise the stakes. Build the second act with dramatic beats, or **action points**, toward a major plot point, that spins the story with momentum into the third act. Explore new territory. Think outside the box.*

* * *

ACT TWO – CARD #4 – (the Confrontation)

LATER THAT MORNING

Sergei and Mark are sitting beside the diesel ENGINE covered in perspiration and grease. Sergei is adjusting an old FLYWHEEL that should be replaced.

> SERGEI
> This was one of the reasons for the bank
> loan that Nik was counting on. We didn't want
> to go to sea without replacing parts like this.
> (uses his wrench)
> By the look of the flywheel and this old diesel
> they've both seen better days.

Sergei now adjusts a pulley beside the worn flywheel.

> MARK
> Can we depend on it?

> SERGEI
> *Mo'zhit-bit.'* With faith and a great deal
> of luck, who knows?

LATER THAT AFTERNOON

Nikolai is applying a canvas patch to his antiquated DIVE SUIT, in addition to other patches. His brass DIVING HELMET also shows years of wear and tear. Mark has just finished cutting a patch and hands it to Nikolai. He carefully smears it with a black adhesive compound and applies it to the suit.

                    MARK
            You really trust this suit?

                   NIKOLAI
                    (nods)
            I have for over thirty years.

He adjusts the patch and looks up with a twinkle in his eye.

                   NIKOLAI
            I'll make a deal with you. When we find
            the gold... I'll buy one of your father's
            Newtsuits with my share.

                    MARK
            You believe the gold's really there?

                   NIKOLAI
            It better be or we're in for a lot of trouble.

Sergei enters the scene, while wiping his greasy hands with a rag.

                   SERGEI
            There's a call for you, Mark. You can take it
            in the wheelhouse.

                    MARK
            I bet it's my dad calling again.

                   SERGEI
            I don't think so, it's a woman's voice.
                    (playful)
            And she sounds pretty sexy.

                                        DISSOLVE TO:

IN MARK'S CABIN

early that evening, he is now neatly dressed in a sport jacket and slacks. While brushing his hair in front of a mirror he begins practicing some basic Russian.

> MARK
> *Dobry vyecher*... Good evening.

He bows slightly with an imaginary reply.

> MARK
> *Khorosho spaseebo*... Fine, thanks.
> (thinks for a moment)
> *Khateetye...lee...vy*.. Would you like...
> ah... nuts!

Mark goes blank. He searches through his luggage beside the bunk. He finds his English/Russian DICTIONARY and looks up the word.

> MARK
> Aaah..*tantsyevat'*

He smiles at the thought and slowly pronounces the word.

> MARK
> *Tantsyevat* ...to dance?

Mark strikes a dance pose just as the SOUND of Sergei's truck horn interrupts his performance. He checks his watch, then grabs a tie from his closet and leaves.

DISSOLVE TO:

SERGEI'S TRUCK

moves quickly along the coastal highway as a golden SUNSET shimmers across the calm waters of the Gulf of Tallinn.

INSIDE THE TRUCK CAB

Mark attempts to make a perfect knot in his tie, but fails. He starts over again.

SERGEI
Is this lady a good looker?

MARK
I think so. She's tall and blonde.

SERGEI
Most Estonian women are. They're closely
related to the Finns by their language.

MARK
Their language?

Mark pulls his tie apart and reties it for the third time, feeling frustrated and a little
nervous that he is about to see Kalin again.

SERGEI
If she's Estonian it's going to be real touchy
with you practicing your Russian on her.

MARK
(swallows nervously)
You're right. I think I'm in big trouble, Sergei.

SERGEI
(grins)
I knew that before we started.

DISSOLVE TO:

SOMETIME LATER ON NOORUSE STREET

as the truck drives along the cobblestone street. It passes under an ancient stone
ARCHWAY, constructed as part of the medieval town, and enters the main street.

MARK (v.o.)
She said the bookstore was just after the
archway... on the second corner.

INSIDE THE TRUCK CAB

as the vehicle pulls up in front of the PEGASUS BOOKSTORE.

SERGEI

We shove off on the high tide at eight bells.
So don't get keel-hauled and blow it, sailor.
Just make sure you're back before we sail.

MARK

Don't worry, I'll be there.

Mark straightens his tie for the last time, steps out of the truck and heads toward the bookstore without looking back. Sergei watches for a moment, then leaves.

DISSOLVE TO:

INSIDE THE PEGASUS BOOKSTORE

all of the tables and chairs are taken. A young MAN, at the back of the room on a small STAGE, is reading a poem by Yevgeny Yevtushenko, over a microphone from a book. The room is dead silent and full of cigarette smoke.

YOUNG MAN

I'll lift an oar and lure a breeze to sail me,
unannounced to sea. I'll drop beneath the
cloudy night and hug the thunder of his
breast, till all is dark forgetfulness.

MARK

enters the bookstore. He looks around then moves along the wall to sit on a bar stool. He appears impressed with the young man's dramatic reading.

YOUNG MAN (v.o.)

And dreams of things that come and go
upon the sighing of a pillow made of
porpoises at rest. Her ship gained snowy
sail at that, cupped a breeze and drew her
on a sharp tack to the sea...

CUT TO:

MARK'S P.O.V. OF THE YOUNG MAN

who now closes his notebook, and finishes the poem from memory.

104

YOUNG MAN
I whispered words I soon forgot and turned
with empty eyes from what I might have had
of life, but for the sea. And felt the fact drop
like a hook that caught and drew a moan
from me. What will I ever say of life to ears
that heard the sea?

He takes a short bow and the room breaks into a loud applause.

CUT TO:

MARK

joins in the applause just as KALIN appears.

KALIN
I see you found your way here.

MARK
Your directions were very good.

KALIN
I have to run an errand. I hope you
don't mind.

Kalin leads him through the smoke-filled room toward a back door.

MARK
What about the poetry reading?

KALIN
They go on all night. We can always come
back later, if you want.

CUT TO:

AN ALLEY BEHIND THE CAFÉ

Kalin approaches a ZIL convertible. There are two boxes of BOOKS in the back seat
beside a PICNIC BASKET. She opens the door and climbs in. Mark joins her.

                            MARK
                    It's a great night for a drive.

                            KALIN
                    It's also a great night for a picnic.

Mark is thrown off guard and laughs.

                            KALIN
                    Why do you laugh?

                            MARK
                    I thought I was coming to a poetry reading
                    in a book store, now we're going on a picnic.
                    This is really crazy, but I'm enjoying it.

                            KALIN
                    You had something else in mind?

The convertible pulls out of the alley and joins the local traffic.

                            MARK (v.o.)
                    Actually, I was thinking of dancing.

                            KALIN (v.o.)
                    We might do that too.

                                              SLOW DISSOLVE TO:

SOMETIME LATER KALIN'S CAR

turns off the NARVA HIGHWAY and they enter a tree-lined entrance to a large wooded
PARK. The setting SUN is barely visible on the horizon.

MOMENTS LATER THE CAR

comes to a stop outside a magnificent PALACE, set among the ancient oaks. Mark
looks up in awe at the stately two-story residence constructed of fieldstone with large
leaded windows. He helps her to carry the books toward the entrance.

                            MARK
                    What is this place?

KALIN

It was Tzar Peter the Great's summer palace,
but it's now a museum for the city. We have
been collecting children's books to help them
restock one part of the library.

The pleasant SOUNDS of someone playing a Jean Sibelius Concerto on a piano are
heard from an open window nearby, as they arrive at the front door.

CUT TO:

MARK'S P.O.V. OF THE ROYAL COAT-OF-ARMS

of Tzar Peter the Great is handsomely carved into the wooden door. Mark reaches out
and runs his hand over the crest.

CUT TO:

BESIDE THE ENTRANCE

Kalin rings an ornate DOORBELL. The SOUNDS of the piano suddenly stop. A moment later, a distinguished looking white-haired WOMAN opens the door.

WOMAN
(smiling)
Kalin, how nice to see you.

KALIN
Good evening Natalya.

INSIDE THE PALACE HALLWAY

Kalin and Mark enter a magnificent interior filled with TAPESTRIES and crystal
CHANDELIERS. The vaulted CEILING is covered in nautical MURALS of sailing
ships. Natalya motions Mark and Kalin to put their box of books on a hall table.

KALIN
This is my friend Mark Fletcher.

NATALYA
It's nice to meet you.

MARK

It's nice to be here.
(looking around)
What a fabulous place.

NATALYA

Thank you, we're still trying to raise funds
to restore most of the Tzar's original murals.
(to Kalin)
I'm practicing for a recital next week, so
if you don't mind, I'll go back to my piano.

KALIN

Please do. We'll put the books in the library.

THE GRAND STAIRWAY

as Kalin leads Mark up the stairs of white marble, both carrying the book boxes. The
SOUNDS of the piano echo along the grand hallway, from far below.

KALIN

This Palace has been one of my favorite places.
My mother used to bring me here when I was
just a little girl, during the summer months.

MOMENTS LATER

they enter the grand DRAWING ROOM. The room is sparsely furnished, but still
imposing, with oriental rugs and a massive fireplace. A life-size PAINTING of Peter
the Great, a most commanding figure, hangs above the fireplace mantle.

CUT TO:

MARK'S P.O.V. OF PETER THE GREAT

stylishly dressed in a colorful naval uniform and mounted on a white horse.

CUT TO:

KALIN

joins Mark at the fireplace, who continues to admire the massive painting.

KALIN

Peter was a man of many interests. While he
was building this palace he became fascinated
in Baltic amber and collected it in all shapes and
sizes. In fact, he created a very special room
just for his amber collection.

MARK

Is that collection still here?

KALIN

(shakes her head)
It was taken by the Nazis in World War II,
during the occupation. It was a priceless
collection and a great loss to our country.

MARK

They took it back to Germany?

KALIN

No, the collection didn't leave the country.
They shipped it down the coastline to the port
of Konigsberg. It was apparently hidden in
the grottos under the city.

MARK

Didn't the allies find it?

KALIN

Nobody found it. Toward the end of the war
the S.S. blew up the dikes and flooded the
city before they left. It has never been found.

Mark is moved by Kalin's story. He shakes his head sadly.

DISSOLVE TO:

SOMETIME LATER IN THE PALACE LIBRARY

Mark is helping Kalin with the children's BOOKS. Kalin is carefully placing them
on the appropriate shelves from a tall wooden LADDER.

MARK

What happens at your bookstore besides
you and your mother selling books?

KALIN

It's where the Estonian Writer's Club meets.
Tonight was our weekly reading of poetry.
The group was created in 1864 to preserve
our written culture.

Mark brings the second box of books over to the ladder.

KALIN

You have to understand we've had a very
long history of invasion and domination
in this country.

MARK

Didn't the Vikings come here?

KALIN

They invaded us in the ninth century followed
by the German knights; then the Polish nobility
looking for land and serfs. Later it was Russian
Czars such as Peter the Great. All looking for an
ice-free port on the Baltic Sea.

MARK

Were they all writers in your store tonight?

KALIN

Some writers... but mostly people that realize
this is our last chance as a nation. History will
not give us another. We were forced into the
Soviet system in 1939, and occupied by the
Russians. But Glasnost has changed all that.
We're free again.

She looks over at Mark, slightly embarrassed and smiles.

KALIN

I must sound like a patriotic radical to you.

110

MARK

No... you sound like a woman with a great
deal of love for your country... I like that.

As she reaches for a book from the pile that Mark is holding, a small book slides off
and falls at Mark's feet. He picks it up and glances at the title on the cover.

MARK

Lewis Carroll. I remember reading this.

He flips through the pages, like discovering an old friend, to a familiar verse.

MARK

The sun was shining on the sea,
Shining with all his might:
He did his very best to make
The billows smooth and bright-
And this was odd, because it was
The middle of the night.

They both laugh and he hands the book up to Kalin.

KALIN

Tell me about your grandfather. Anatoli
tells me that he was a salvage diver for
the Baltic Fleet.

MARK
(nods)
Nik was with the fleet for twenty-five years.

KALIN

Which side of the family is he on?

MARK

My mother's side. She met my father when
he was in the Navy, on a tour of the Baltic.

KALIN

How did she escape the communists?

MARK

Through Finland with my uncle. She was
only eighteen years old.

KALIN

She lives with you in Canada?

MARK

(matter-of-fact)
She died six years ago.

KALIN

I'm sorry to hear that.

Mark remains silent. He takes her hand and helps her down the ladder.

DISSOLVE TO:

IN THE PALACE BALLROOM

moonlight fills the leaded windows sending long shafts of soft light across the baronial
walls that are covered in faded seascapes. The piano SOUNDS continue. Mark and
Kalin are sitting on pillows in the middle of the parquet floor. They are both eating
from the open picnic basket and drinking from two wine glasses.

MARK

It's a perfect place for a picnic.

KALIN

I'm sure Tzar Peter would agree.

Mark refills their wine glasses.

MARK

Where did you grow up?

KALIN

I was born in Tallinn, and we lived in
St. Petersburg and Moscow for a while.
Then my father was posted to the Soviet
Embassy in Canada, when I was eight.

MARK

In Canada?

KALIN

Yes, in Ottawa. I spent four years in a school
for embassy children where I learned to speak
English. I returned to live in Tallinn with my
mother when I was twelve.

MARK

What happened to your father?

Kalin looks up and forces a sad smile

KALIN

He stayed behind in Canada and remarried.
We haven't heard from him since. It was very
difficult for us with the KGB and their many
investigations into his defection...
(takes a beat)
That's all in the past. My mother and I are
happy and we have our bookstore to run.

Mark decides to change the subject. He reaches out and takes her hand.

MARK

I'm been practicing my Russian, but I'm
afraid I don't know any Estonian, yet.

KALIN
(amused)
That's alright... try me.

MARK

Khateetye leevy...tantsyevat?

Kalin smiles and stands up. Mark joins her and she offers her hand.

KALIN

Yes, I would love to dance.

Kalin moves into his arms. They dance across the ballroom to the SOUNDS of the distant PIANO. Mark is somewhat awkward at first, and then as they begin to relax in each other's arms they soon glide effortlessly across the moonlit space.

DISSOLVE TO:

MANY HOURS LATER KALIN'S CAR

drives through the gateway into the SALVAGE YARD just as the SUNRISE rims the distant horizon. The convertible comes to a stop beside the old salvage tug.

KALIN

Anatoli was right.

MARK

Right about what?

KALIN

He said we'd have a great time together.

MARK
(nods)

He was right...

She opens her purse and pulls out an AMBER nugget, fastened to a bronze chain.

KALIN

I thought you'd like to wear this on the
dive. It's a talisman of Baltic amber.

She hands it to him and Mark examines it.

KALIN

It belonged to my great grandfather. He wore
it throughout his years in the Crimean War.

Mark holds it up to the sunlight. It appears to glow from within.

KALIN

In Homer's Odyssey he writes of Ulysses
wearing a talisman of amber to enhance
his power. Maybe it will work for you.

114

She fastens the chain around his neck. Their faces remain close, eyes locked.

MARK
Thank you for this...

Kalin leans forward and kisses Mark gently on the lips. He returns the gesture with a kiss that makes Kalin squirm with pleasure.

KALIN
I'll see you when you get back. Be careful.

Just before Mark steps out of the car she takes his arm.

KALIN
Don't forget this.

She holds up the Lewis Carroll BOOK of poetry. He takes it and steps out.

CAMERA WIDENS:

He pauses to watch Kalin's car pass through the gates and into the SUNRISE. Mark is on cloud nine as he bounces up the tug's gangplank.

DISSOLVE TO:

* * *

*Our **developing plot** is the search for a lost treasure. That plot is what drives the main action of our story, from the very beginning to the end. However, our **subplot** is about relationships. The relationships between Mark, his father and Nikolai. There's even a strong, ongoing relationship between the <u>sea</u> and those who chose to seek their fortunes from her, as expressed in this story.*

*We have now introduced Kalin into this interesting mix. She takes Mark to Peter the Great's summer palace for a fascinating evening among the splendor of a bygone era, and we learn of the Tzar's loss of a priceless treasure of Baltic amber. It is a perfect setting for their first date. It opens up the film visually in contrast to Nikolai's world. And Mark is now wearing an amber **talisman** from Kalin; this lucky charm is an ongoing symbol of their relationship and a foreshadowing of things to come. I'm sure our audience is waiting for the result of this romantic encounter and wondering how these new dynamics will shape the future of our story.*

It is also a good time to discuss an ingredient known as the **back-story**. When I was producing a daytime drama called "Generations" at NBC in their Burbank studios in California my weekly meetings with our writing staff always included a back-story scenario. That was also true when I later produced "Family Passions" in Canada for Germany's NDF (Neue Deutsche Filmgesellschaft mbH), along with the CTV Network in Toronto, Canada.

In such cases, the backbone of every daytime drama ever written is the back-story. Without a solid back-story the series will lack depth in your leading characters and will also lack much of the character-driven content that is needed to enhance the overall storyline. However, a feature film usually tries to eliminate much of the back-story because of the limited timeframe, whereas a daytime drama will thrive on a back-story and finds it necessary in a long-term series of any consequence.

Agnes Nixon, the acknowledged master of daytime dramas and the creator of "One Life to Live," "Search for Tomorrow," "All My Children," "Another World," "The Guiding Light," and "As the World Turns" believes that much of the ongoing story will always depend on the back story. Situations change, human nature does not. Her fictional characters may suffer in each story from a number of society's daily ailments but their real problems are born in their soul. Her secret? She always knows who the character is before she starts writing any long-term story concept. Her characters are characters that have a history, all with a back-story. It's a lesson well learned and one that can provide depth to any story, sometimes revealed in **flashbacks**, though used very sparingly.

* * *

ACT TWO – CARD #5

MUCH LATER THAT MORNING

the powerful TUGBOAT rides the gentle swells of the BALTIC SEA.

INSIDE THE WHEEL HOUSE

Nikolai is at the WHEEL while Mark carefully studies the distant horizon with a pair of BINOCULARS.

NIKOLAI
You should be sighting the island any minute.

116

MARK

There's nothing on the horizon yet but a thin
layer of fog.

Sergei enters the wheel house with a pleased expression on his face.

SERGEI

I've made adjustments on the flywheel to
reduce the vibration. It looks good for now.

NIKOLAI

Sergei, take the wheel, I'll check the chart.

Sergei takes the wheel as Nikolai steps to the CHART TABLE. Mark joins him. Nikolai
points to a small penciled DOT on the CHART.

NIKOLAI

That's where we need to be.

Nikolai takes the parallel RULES and lays them on the chart.

NIKOLAI

Sergei, what time is it?

Sergei pulls out his submariner's pocket WATCH, with a large sweep hand, and carefully calculates the time down to the last second.

SERGEI

It's eleven-twenty... two.

Nikolai takes the parallel rules and strikes a fine LINE to the dot and reads out the
bearing on the CHART.

NIKOLAI
(calculating)
With a slight south-west current, we'll be
on our site around twelve.

MARK
(studying the depth)
It's over two hundred feet at that point.

NIKOLAI

That's right, the freighter is resting on a ridge
at a depth a lttle over 73 meters according to our
depth finder readings.

MARK

Was it torpedoed?

NIKOLAI

It's uncertain... it went down in 1945 and
the reports were very confusing.

SERGEI

There was also a report that it collided during
a thick fog with another vessel.

NIKOLAI

That's another story but nobody knows for
certain. It's really become a mystery ship.

SERGEI

There were no survivors reported. When we
searched the naval records in St. Petersburg
for the files, they were all missing.

MARK

Isn't that rather odd?

SERGEI

Not in this country it isn't.

MARK

So we'll be the first to board her...

NIKOLAI

We'll be the first. And I'm going to be the first
to visit the galley and make us some fresh coffee.

Nikolai leaves by a side door as Mark scans the horizon.

SERGEI

I don't suppose you got much sleep last night.

                    MARK
              (matter-of-fact)
        No, I didn't. But I had a great time. Kalin
        is really wonderful.

                    SERGEI
        You keep telling me that.

Mark shows Sergei the TALISMAN that hangs from his neck.

                    MARK
        She gave me this talisman for good luck.

                    SERGEI
                  (ribs him)
        She certainly has excellent taste... when
        it comes to her amber.

They both laugh, but Mark appears a little embarrassed.

                                        DISSOLVE TO:

SOMETIME LATER

the tug cuts a sweeping arc as it leans into a starboard turn.

INSIDE THE WHEEL HOUSE

Nikolai is guiding the tug while concentrating on the movements from the recording
FATHOMETER as Sergei and Mark look on.

                    SERGEI
        It's twelve-fifteen, we should be getting
        real close to our dive site.

                                        CUT TO:

NIKOLAI'S P.O.V. OF THE FATHOMETER

as the electronic instrument scribes the ocean floor with a thin black sweeping line
etched on the scrolling PAPER.

NIKOLAI (v.o.)
The next pass should do it.

The straight pattern suddenly jumps and begins to print out the OUTLINE of a three hundred and fifty foot VESSEL onto the moving paper.

CUT TO:

INSIDE THE WHEEL HOUSE

as Nikolai eases the throttle control back. Both Sergei and Mark are excited.

SERGEI
That's it! Right on target.

NIKOLAI
Let's get hooked in for the dive.

Sergei and Mark head toward the exit when suddenly the RADIO SPEAKER breaks silence and the static-filled SOUNDS of a distorted transmission is heard.

OPERATOR (v.o.)
Mayday! Mayday! This is the fishing boat
Tammsaare! We are fighting a fire! Mayday!
Mayday! (more static) We are on fire! We
are twenty-two kilometers east of Kardla!

NIKOLAI
Sergei get the glasses. That boat's about
two kilometers south of us!

Sergei begins to scan the southern horizon with the binoculars.

SERGEI
(sights it)
It's off our starboard bow ten degrees.
You can see the smoke from the fire.

Nikolai immediately spins the WHEEL all the way, while simultaneously hitting the throttle. The tugboat heels under the torque, and then straightens. Sergei can't believe that they are abandoning the dive.

120

SERGEI

What're you doing? Are you crazy, Nik?
We're sitting on a fortune in gold, you can't
leave here now!

Nikolai ignores him and pushes the throttle all the way.

NIKOLAI
(firm)
They're seamen just like us and they need
our help. And that's where we're going!

CUT TO:

THE ENGINE ROOM BILGE

as the main SEACOCK moves slightly under the increased pressure on the hull. Three
of the five BOLTS are clearly CUT IN HALF. The two remaining BOLTS twist slightly,
but hold. Seawater begins to spray from the weakened FLANGE.

CUT TO:

INSIDE THE WHEEL HOUSE

Nikolai grabs the MICROPHONE to the ship's RADIO.

NIKOLAI
Hello Tammsaare... this is the tug Baltic Star.
We have sighted you. And we are on our way!
I repeat, we are on our way!

Nikolai looks over at Sergei who slowly nods his understanding. He steps up to the
wheel beside Nikolai, feeling a little awkward.

SERGEI
(forthright)
You're right Nik, it's your call. They need
our help and we should definitely be there.

THE BALTIC STAR

noticeably begins to roll in the swells as it pushes toward a thick cloud of SMOKE on
the distant horizon at flank speed.

MOMENTS LATER, SERGEI AND MARK

are both standing on the outer BRIDGE as the tug approaches from downwind riding
the heavy ground-swell in.

MARK
(pointing)
There she is, I can see her bow!

CUT TO:

MARK'S P.O.V. OF THE TAMMSAARE

as FLAMES and SMOKE belch from the crippled 80-ton fishing boat. A lone
FISHERMAN onboard attempts to battle the fire, while three FISHERMEN, all
wearing life jackets, are already floating in the oil-clad sea.

SERGEI (v.o.)
She could explode any minute!

MARK (v.o.)
There's still someone onboard!

CUT TO:

MARK AND SERGEI

quickly move down to the main DECK. The fisherman onboard continues to fight the
fire. Sergei picks up a BULLHORN and activates it.

SERGEI
Poneemahyetye ly vy? You must abandon
the ship immediately!

Suddenly a piercing EXPLOSION rips through the listing hull.

CUT TO:

MARK'S P.O.V. OF THE EXPLOSION

as flaming pieces shower the tug with burning DEBRIS. And just as the swirling
smoke clears the boat for a moment there is no sign of the fisherman.

122

                        MARK (v.o.)
          Where'd he go?

                                                        CUT TO:

THE TUG

slowly circles the burning fishing boat, through a thick cloud of black smoke, as the
cargo area continues to EXPLODE with flames.

MARK AND SERGEI

help two SURVIVORS onboard. Then they pull the third fishermen from the sea.

                                                        CUT TO:

MARK'S P.O.V. OF THE DEAD FISHERMAN IN HIS ARMS

He is still wearing a pea jacket under his badly burned life jacket. His frightened face
is covered in oil and grease.

                                                        CUT TO:

MARK

suddenly recognizes the young fisherman. It is the same young man that he saw reciting his poetry at the Estonian Writer's Club.

                        MARK
          My God... how can that be?

Mark realizes he is looking at the face of death.

                        MARK
          I just saw him last night reciting poetry
          at the bookstore and he was alive!

Sergei grabs Mark by the shoulder to shake him out of it.

                        SERGEI
          Mark! There's still someone left onboard
          the fishing boat. We need to get to him!

Mark places the fisherman's lifeless body aside and turns to the rail.

INSIDE THE WHEEL HOUSE NIKOLAI

guides the tug through islands of burning debris. He cautiously maneuvers in very close to the remains of the burning boat.

BLACK SMOKE

clouds the tug's bow. Mark shields his watery eyes as he steps toward the bow to search the burning SEA for any signs of life.

                         MARK
               Hello... Hel-loo...

Faint at first but still audible, he is sure he hears a voice.

                       VOICE (v.o.)
               Over here!

                                                    CUT TO:

MARK'S P.O.V. OF THE BURNING FISHING BOAT

through a break in the smoke. Mark can see a FIGURE still onboard holding onto the smoking bow, some fifty yards ahead.

                                                    CUT TO:

MARK

waves to Nikolai in the wheelhouse.

                         MARK
               Nik, there's someone on the bow!

Nikolai immediately cuts back on the tug's power. Inch by inch the tug closes the distance as SMOKE and FLAMES continue to fill the air all around them. Mark leans over the rail and shouts at the fisherman.

                         MARK
               We can't get much closer! You'll have
               to swim for it!

THE FISHERMAN

appears injured and he is not wearing a life jacket.

> FISHERMAN
>
> No... I can't swim!

The sinking boat continues to burn all around him. Sergei joins Mark at the rail and he too shouts to the stranded fisherman.

> SERGEI
>
> Take it easy! When our bow swings in,
> it'll be close enough to jump onboard!

The tug continues to get closer as the seas proceed to roll under her hull, raising her high above the burning boat, then slipping back. The fisherman climbs over the rail, ready to jump onto the tug, as the tug slowly closes the gap.

> SERGEI
>
> Get ready to jump... now JUMP!

The terrified fisherman releases the rail just as a rogue WAVE curls under the burning hulk. He loses his balance and is PITCHED forward into the SEA. Nikolai instantly REVERSES the tug.

CUT TO:

MARK'S P.O.V. OF THE OCEAN

while looking for the fisherman. It feels like an eternity before the fisherman reappears, gasping for air and floundering to stay afloat on the oily surface.

> MARK (v.o.)
>
> I've got him!

CUT TO:

MARK

without hesitation, jumps overboard into the sea. He lands near the fisherman and grabs him just as a giant swell rolls over them. The both disappear below the burning oil-laden surface.

SERGEI

saw Mark jump overboard and runs to the rail with a survival RING in his hand.

SERGEI
(frantic)
Mark!... Mark!... Where are you?

They suddenly break the surface and Sergei tosses the ring. Mark grabs it and drags the bewildered fisherman through the choppy seas to the side of the tug. They are pulled onboard just as another explosion rips through the fishing boat.

THE BALTIC STAR

shudders as the derelict fishing boat suddenly CRASHES into its hull. Nikolai desperately backs away under full power.

SERGEI

helps Mark to his feet, wet and covered in oil and they hug.

SERGEI
My God, I thought we lost you.

Mark helps the fisherman, who is still unsteady. He shakes Mark's hand firmly.

FISHERMAN
You saved my life... I won't forget you!

CUT TO:

CLOUDS OF OILY STEAM

begin to rise out of the ENGINE ROOM HATCH. Sergei is the first to see it and runs to investigate. He steps into the hatch and disappears into the steam.

INSIDE THE ENGINE ROOM

Sergei finds it flooded. He shields his eyes from the blinding oil vapors in the room, while using a FLASHLIGHT to find the source of the flooding.

CUT TO:

SERGEI'S P.O.V. OF THE MAIN SEACOCK

and the SAWED BOLTS. The sea is flooding the compartment and the valve is out of reach in the lower cavity of the bilge.

CUT TO:

IN THE ENGINE ROOM

Sergei activates an antiquated switch and an auxiliary PUMP comes to life. Then he turns to a TELEPHONE on the wall.

> SERGEI
> Nik, the main seacock has been sabotaged.
> We're taking on water. It's separating from
> the hull under the engine bed.

INSIDE THE WHEEL HOUSE

Nikolai listens to his report on the INTERCOM. Sergi's voice is barely audible above the engine noise as Mark enters the wheelhouse.

> SERGEI (v.o.)
> It's underwater, impossible to reach and the
> water-pump can hardly keep up. Our night
> visitor did a good job of sawing through all
> the bolts but two. That's all that's holding her.

> NIKOLAI
> I've already reported our situation to the Coast
> Guard. They know we're coming in with the
> fishermen we saved.
>   (not wanting to ask)
> How much time do we have?

> SERGEI (v.o.)
> At this rate of flooding maybe two hours.
>   (takes a beat)
> Then I'm afraid we'll be swimming home.

NIKOLAI
See if you can wedge something against
the valve to slow down the pressure.

MARK
(angry)
Who'd do this to us?

NIKOLAI
The real question is why!

DISSOLVE TO:

SOMETIME LATER

the tugboat, now low in the water, is nudged shoreward by a following sea. Half-a-mile offshore, she swings in line with the channel.

IN THE ENGINE ROOM

Sergei has wedged the VALVE with a length of steel channel, and wood blocks against the shifting base of the flooding seacock. He crosses the compartment in water up to his ankles to tap on the dial of the pump's wavering PRESSURE GAUGE. The needle is slowly falling. He rechecks the squealing WATER PUMP.

SERGEI
Just keep running, and I'll give you a
new set of bearings when we get home!

Sergei crosses back to look at the SEACOCK and to check on the wood blocks. Water continues to FLOOD into the steam-filled compartment.

DISSOLVE TO:

SOMETIME LATER

the tug enters the channel, close to the point that separates a BEACH from the inner harbor. Her stern deck is awash, responding sluggishly to the helm.

A COAST GUARD HELICOPTER

circles the tug a number of times, then returns to the mainland.

INSIDE THE WHEEL HOUSE

Nikolai is having great difficulty managing the wheel. The tug is losing speed as the diesel strains to keep up. He uses the INTERCOM.

> NIKOLAI
> Sergei, how are we doing?

> SERGEI (v.o.)
> The water pump is really in bad shape.

> NIKOLAI
> Can you hang on for fifteen minutes?

> SERGEI (v.o.)
> Negative. The flooding is getting worse.

Nikolai considers his answer, and then he makes a decision.

> NIKOLAI
> We'll never make the wharf at this rate.
> I think our best chance is to beach her.

> SERGEI (v.o.)
> If that's the only way to save her, let's go!

> NIKOLAI
> Mark! Grab a life jacket and give Sergei
> a hand, but be ready to abandon ship!

THE BALTIC STAR

as a white frothing sea breaks continuously over the stern rail, driving the tugboat lower and lower with every assault.

INSIDE THE ENGINE ROOM

the water is now knee deep as Mark enters. The air reeks of diesel oil and the noise is deafening. The FLYWHEEL and PULLEYS shower the compartment with water from the incoming sea.

SERGEI

is carefully pouring the remains of a CAN of oil on the water-pump's screeching PULLEY. Mark quickly wades over to his side.

MARK
How can I help you?

Sergei hands Mark the oil CAN and points at the smoking PULLY.

SERGEI
Just keep it oiled!

Suddenly without warning the SEACOCK tears away from the hull. A four-inch COLUMN of seawater explodes into the engine room. Mark and Sergei scramble through the water and up the ladder to escape the flooding.

CUT TO:

* * *

We have now dramatically upped the stakes. And there will be many more major obstacles for our trio to overcome, as we head towards the mid-point of our story. I'm sure the bank is waiting to liquidate Nikolai's assets, as soon as he docks, if he makes it. Without banking support he is left with his antiquated diving equipment and an aging tugboat that needs major repairs.

Gorzenko, however, has successfully crippled the tug, at this point, leaving them to the mercy of the sea. The confrontations are now coming fast and furious and the intensity of these actions will only increase. Dramatic conflict feeds the flames of character development. Mark, Nikolai and Sergei are now facing a life-or-death situation. They need all of their fortitude to survive this day.

* * *

ACT TWO – CARD #6

INSIDE THE WHEEL HOUSE

Nikolai throttles full forward and grabs the LOUD-HAILER.

NIKOLAI
Everyone on deck! We're going to beach
her, so hold on. Here we go!
(spins the heavy wheel)
Come'n girl, don't tear your bottom out!

THE BALTIC STAR

with her aft gunnels almost submerged begins a slow starboard turn. Black SMOKE belches from her stack as the turn sharpens, burying her rail. A Coast Guard BOAT follows the struggling tug at a distance.

ON THE BEACH

members of the COASTAL RESCUE stand by their equipment. A FIRE ENGINE and an AMBULANCE arrives on the beach. A group of spectators, standing along the shoreline watch the strange maneuvering of the crippled tug.

KALIN'S CAR

appears on the road opposite the beach. The SOUND of a NEWS REPORT is heard on her car radio as she pulls up, and quickly parks.

ANNOUNCER (v.o.)
The Baltic Star, a salvage tug, reported
sighting the burning fishing boat Tammsaare
at twelve-thirty this afternoon according to
a report from the local Coast Guard. There
is not a confirmed report on survivors at this
point but we do know that the Tammsaare
has been destroyed by fire. A further report
will be given at...

Kalin flips off the radio, jumps from the car, and runs down to the shoreline.

INSIDE THE WHEEL HOUSE

Sergei joins Nikolai. It is a tense moment as Nikolai tries to get every revolution out of the screaming diesel engine.

MARK AT THE BOW RAILING

supports himself against a BOLLARD as he looks toward the beach, and the rescue crews that are waiting. The fishermen brace themselves ready for the collision as four-hundred tons of wood and steel fast approach the shoreline.

KALIN

shades her eyes from the sun, to watch the floundering tugboat fast approaching.

CUT TO:

KALIN'S P.O.V. OF THE BALTIC STAR

as the crippled tug suddenly hits bottom. The sharp impact shudders through the massive framework. Pieces of equipment on the DECK break away and tumble into the sea. The tug lunges on, propelled by her enormous momentum. A large plume of white sand billows in the tug's wake. Great clouds of swirling steam suddenly EXPLODE from the engine room doorway.

CUT TO:

INSIDE THE WHEEL HOUSE

Nikolai is hurled against the wheel. Sergei crashes into the forward bulkhead. Charts, navigational instruments, coffee cups and a chair fly through the air. The overhead radio crashes through the forward window spewing glass everywhere.

THE CAREENING TUG

finally buries itself some twenty yards from the SHORELINE at a forty-five degree angle. Steam and black oily SMOKE continue to fill the air.

KALIN AND THE SPECTATORS

begin to follow two members of the Coastal Rescue Squad as they wade into the shallow sea toward the tugboat.

MARK

climbs into the wheelhouse. Sergei is badly bruised as he regains his feet. Nikolai is lying unconscious under the ship's wheel. Mark kneels down beside the old man and gently lifts his head. A smear of blood streaks the corner of his mouth .

                              SERGEI
                             (groggy)
              Is Nik alright?

                               MARK
              I don't know.

At that moment Nikolai opens his eyes, and looks up at Mark in a daze.

                             NIKOLAI
                    Is everything... okay?

Mark begins to tear as he gently cradles his grandfather in his arms.

                               MARK
                    We made it, Nik. Everything is going
                    to be okay, I promise you.

KALIN

wades through the ankle deep water toward the tug. The Rescue Squad stands by as
Sergei appears at the rail and drops a rope LADDER over the side.

TWO MEDICS

immediately climb onboard and evacuate the two fishermen.

NIKOLAI

is brought out on a stretcher and lowered over the side by the medics. Sergei and Mark
descend the ladder to help the medics.

                              SERGEI
                    How is he?

                               MEDIC
                    We need to let the doctor take a good look
                    at him. He could have internal injuries.

Nikolai looks up at Sergei and forces a disappointed smile.

NIKOLAI
I guess we can tell comrade Tulchinsky
where to collect his boat now.

SERGEI
(emotional)
Nik, you did what you had to do. I'm just
glad we're all alive.

The Medics carry the stretcher toward the shoreline. Sergei puts his arm around Mark,
looking very tired and depressed, and they follow the medics.

SERGEI
If you need me... I'll be at the Karolina
Bar getting drunk.
(leans closer to Mark)
And watch your back. Someone doesn't
want us onboard The Prince of Russia.

AT THE AMBULANCE

a crowd of spectators watches the proceedings as Nikolai is loaded. GORZENKO
suddenly appears and approaches one of the medics at the stretcher. He looks down
at Nikolai, who is resting with his eyes closed.

GORZENKO
Is he going to live?

MEDIC
We don't know.

They slide the stretcher into the ambulance and close the doors.

GORZENKO

looks toward the sea and the beached tug that is still spewing black smoke, with a
look of satisfaction on his face, then turns and leaves.

KALIN

joins Mark whose clothing is oil-stained and charred. He is glad to see her. She puts
her arm around him and they wade toward the beach.

KALIN

I'm so glad you're safe.

Mark looks over at her and nods without a word.

DISSOLVE TO:

A FRAMED PHOTOGRAPH

of the *Baltic Star*, when it was first purchased, looking neat and freshly painted.
Nikolai and Sergei are proudly posing for the picture, beside the tugboat.

CAMERA WIDENS:

Nikolai, dressed in a ROBE, reaches out and removes the photograph from the wall
of his STUDY. His movements are slow as he places the photo into a box beside the
chart-table, with other objects of memorabilia. Mark enters the room.

MARK

Nik, what're you doing up? You should
be in bed resting.

NIKOLAI

I feel fine. The doctor x-rayed me, taped
me up and they brought me home. I've had
cracked ribs before... and besides...
(playful)
It only hurts when I move.

MARK

(has to smile)
Well, you haven't lost your sense of humor.

Nikolai sits down with some difficulty, holding his left side with one hand.

NIKOLAI

You were a real hero today, Mark. I'm proud
of what you did. You have the spirit of your
mother. And don't ever lose it.

MARK

We couldn't have done it without you at
the helm, taking care of business.

NIKOLAI

I won't always be at the helm. You'll need
your father's support when I'm not around.

MARK

(sarcastic)

You mean ,Doctor Fletcher.'

NIKOLAI

No, I mean a career naval officer who met
and married my daughter, and made her
extremely happy for the first time in her life.

MARK

(bitter)

Then why didn't he save her from drowning?

NIKOLAI

You can't blame your father for her death.
Nobody knew that she went on a night dive
all by herself, from their research boat.

MARK

(surprised)

She went on a night dive by herself?

NIKOLAI

When she was reported missing your father
was desperate to find her. He spent the night
searching for her.

(slowly shakes his head)

They finally had to force him out of the
water, he was suffering from exhaustion
and hypothermia. He was hospitalized
for two days, and almost died.

MARK

(solemn)

He never told me that.

NIKOLAI

He's never able to talk about it. He blames

himself and always will. It's not fair for you
to blame him on top of that. It was a tragedy.
It's time for you to make amends.

                    MARK
Make amends?

                    NIKOLAI
Yes, try and understand that your father
won't change until you change. You have
to change first.

                    MARK
I don't understand.

                    NIKOLAI
His loss and suffering has been as great
as yours. You need to realize that there is
no one to blame for what happened.
          (puts his arm around Mark)
Your father loved your mother as much
as he loves you, just remember that.

Mark slowly nods, he has nothing to say.

                                        DISSOLVE TO:

LATER THAT NIGHT

Mark and Kalin are sitting in a secluded area among the pine-scented sand DUNES
that overlook the Bay of Tallinn. In the distance, the silhouette of the grounded TUG
can be seen looming high and dry in the draining tide.

                    KALIN
My mother told me about your grandfather.
She said Nikolai was one of our war heroes.
The Nazis could never catch him. As a young
man he was able to ferry underground agents
into the country to sabotage installations.

                    MARK
I heard the same stories from my mother.

KALIN

Those fishermen you saved today are his
people and you showed the courage of your
grandfather when you jumped into the sea.

Mark looks over at Kalin sadly recalling the tragedy.

MARK

One of the dead fishermen was the
person I saw reading poetry in your
bookstore... He was my age.

KALIN

His name was Enn Lurich.

MARK

This time last night he was still alive.
Who would ever think that he would
be dead the next day?

KALIN

It's fate. There's no way of ever knowing.

MARK
(angry)
It wasn't fate that destroyed the Baltic Star.

KALIN

I don't understand. The radio report said
that by being in the same area you were able
to save the fishermen... but it didn't explain
why the tug was damaged.

MARK

It was a simple case of sabotage. Sergei
found the bolts cut through on the main sea
valve. It was impossible to repair. The tug
started to take on water almost immediately
after the rescue. We were lucky to even get
her as far as the beach.

KALIN
Who would do such a thing?

MARK
(matter-of-fact)
Someone who doesn't want us to be onboard
that old freighter, that's what we believe.

Mark stands up; he wants to change the subject.

MARK
Let's go for a walk.

He offers her his hand; she takes it and stands up.

DISSOLVE TO:

SOMETIME LATER

the BAY OF TALLINN is shimmering with the midsummer glow. The full MOON
and VENUS hang overhead like ornaments in the indigo night sky.

MARK AND KALIN

are walking barefoot, along the beach, in the out going TIDE.

DISSOLVE TO:

BESIDE THE BALTIC STAR

they move into the shadows of the battered hull. Kalin steps forward into his arms
and they kiss passionately. Mark sweeps her off her feet and carries her through the
surf to the rope LADDER hanging from the rail of the old tugboat.

SLOW FADE TO:

IN THE TUGBOAT CABIN

Kalin is lying beside Mark in a BUNK reading from the Lewis Carroll book of poetry.
CANDLES illuminate the interior. Mark looks relaxed after his near death experience
and is enjoying her companionship.

KALIN

"I weep for you," the Walrus said:
"I deeply sympathize."
With sobs and tears he sorted out
Those of the largest size,
Holding his pocket-handkerchief
Before his streaming eyes.

She looks over at Mark who smiles drowsily back at her.

KALIN

"O Oysters," said the Carpenter,
"You've had a pleasant run!
Shall we be trotting home again?"
But answer came there none-
And this was scarcely odd, because
They'd eaten every one.

She closes the book. Mark is sound asleep with a smile on his face. She takes the
TALISMAN, on a chain from around his neck, and lifts the amber orb to her lips.

KALIN
(whispering)
Thank you for bringing him back.

DISSOLVE TO:

DAYBREAK THE NEXT MORNING

and the tide has drained the BEACH as seagulls sweep overhead. The old salt-washed
tugboat looks like a beached whale, riveted into the sand.

DISSOLVE TO:

INSIDE THE CABIN

sunlight fills the porthole washing the sleeping faces of Kalin and Mark. The cabin
is on a slope and two of the candles are still burning. Kalin stirs and wakes up, and
for a moment she is confused by the slope of the cabin. She looks over at Mark, then
gently runs her hand through his tousled hair.

KALIN
Dobraya ootro... good morning.

140

Mark stirs, but his eyes remain closed. Suddenly the deafening SOUNDS of heavy machinery interrupts their mood. Mark looks out the porthole toward the beach.

CUT TO:

MARK'S P.O.V. OF THREE LARGE TRUCKS

that are fast approaching the tugboat. They are loaded with salvage equipment, pumps, scaffolding and hydraulic jacks, followed by an enormous BULLDOZER.

CUT TO:

INSIDE THE CABIN

Mark swings his naked body from under the blankets to the edge of the sloped bunk and pulls on his shorts.

MARK
We've got visitors!

CUT TO:

* * *

There's nothing like the arrival of a salvage dismantling crew, along with tons of heavy equipment, to interrupt a romantic mood between our two young lovers. Besides this, in the last ten pages we have completed a harrowing rescue of the fishermen at sea, the violent beaching of Nikolai's tugboat, and some important revelations about Mark's mother that Mark never knew. That alone could change Mark's relationship with his father. We have also brought his relationship with Kalin much closer.

*These events also pose some **relief** for our audience before the next dramatic encounter. Time to catch our breath. Like most skillful methods in effective storytelling our audience should be in the dark about what could happen next. It should be a moment in your story when our main characters appear to have no options left. They have reached a dead end. Nothing seems to work.*

However, I'm quite sure that some eventful incident will take place that will trigger a new direction for them to follow. We are not sure of what that will be. This is always an exciting moment for an audience to try and second-guess the storyteller, who, hopefully, has control of the events. Where do we go from here?

* * *

THE TRUCKS AND THE BULLDOZER

come to a stop, within a few yards of the tug. TULCHINSKY steps out of the lead truck, followed by a crew of carpenters and ironworkers.

> TULCHINSKY
> Okay, men, you know why we're here. Get
> your frames under that old tug. I want a float
> platform ready by noon, for the high tide.

The figures of Mark and Kalin now appear on the deck of the tug. They make their way down the rope ladder, into the rising surf.

KALIN AND MARK

arrive on the beach. The workers begin carrying timbers and scaffold toward the tug. Mark and Kalin are met by Tulchinsky. He is dressed in a brand NEW SUIT, with his trousers carefully tucked into a pair of black rubber waders.

> TULCHINSKY
> Good morning.

Tulchinsky tips his crisp new FEDORA to Kalin with a sly smile.

> TULCHINSKY
> I hope we're not disturbing you.

Mark doesn't like this man and his obvious insinuations.

> MARK
> (demanding)
> What're you doing here?

Tulchinsky now recognizes Mark and is surprised to see him.

> TULCHINSKY
> I met with Nikolai this morning and offered
> our services. We intend to patch the hull and
> refloat it, then make repairs for a resale.

MARK

You said we had seventy-two hours.

TULCHINSKY

As I explained to Nikolai, we need to salvage
this tug before it gets battered in the tides,
before we can resume ownership.
(he waves at the tug)
Nobody ever thought it would end up on the
beach like this unattended!

MARK

Did Nik tell you that someone sabotaged
the tug, and that's why this happened?

TULCHINSKY

No, he didn't. And frankly, I'm not concerned
with how it got here. My job is to protect the
bank's property at this time.

MARK

Legally, it's not your property yet.

TULCHINSKY

That really doesn't matter. Your grandfather
became bankrupt when he beached the tug.
The bank now controls his assets whether
you like it or not!

MARK
(angry)
That's a lot of bullshit!

Mark grabs him by the lapels, but the force of his action causes Tulchinsky to stumble
over his own feet, lose his balance, and fall into the wet sand. The workers stop work
to watch the argument. Tulchinsky scrambles to his feet.

TULCHINSKY
I'll have you arrested for this!

Mark ignores his threat and confronts him face on.

MARK

What you don't understand is that my
grandfather is responsible for his own fortunes.
You don't control them! This is a new Baltic
nation and the banks, especially your bank,
should be here to help everyone in this
country to be successful at what they do!

Now all of the workers that have been listening nod in complete agreement.

TULCHINSKY

That's a very capitalistic idea!

Mark realizes that this is a no-win situation with this man.

MARK

No. It's a very humane concepts!

Mark decides to leave, then stops and looks back at Tulchinsky.

MARK

I suggest you learn a few capitalistic ideas,
Tulchinsky, if you want to survive here!

The workers begin to loudly APPLAUD Mark as he strides off along the beach, followed by Kalin. Tulchinsky angrily turns on them.

TULCHINSKY

Get back to work or I'll fire all of you!

CUT TO:

MARK AND KALIN

as they walk briskly along the BEACH toward Kalin's parked car.

KALIN

Mark... you were great!

MARK
(frustrated)
It didn't get us anywhere.

KALIN
(starts to laugh)
You almost ripped the lapels right off his
tacky new suit!

Mark stops dead in his tracks. He looks over at Kalin with a grin on his face.

MARK
His new suit?
(elated)
Kalin you're absolutely wonderful and
I love you for it.

Mark leans over and kisses her. Kalin is stunned by his sudden mad outburst.

KALIN
I don't get it...

MARK
(inspired)
You don't have to... we need to find Sergei
right away, and I need to find a telephone!

DISSOLVE TO:

SOMETIME LATER

Sergei's TRUCK speeds along the coastal HIGHWAY towards St. Petersburg.

SERGEI (v.o.)
(badly hung-over)
So you think this 'Newtsuit' is the answer?

MARK (v.o.)
All I know, is when I talked to Anatoli he
agreed to release the back-up Newtsuit to us
for forty-eight hours, including a dive boat.

SERGEI (v.o.)
The Admiral's protégé seems to be very
generous. But how'd you rate a dive boat?

KALIN (v.o.)
Mark made a deal with him.

SERGEI (v.o.)
What kind of a deal?

MARK (v.o.)
Anatoli needs a little adventure in his life
right now... so he's coming along to operate
the onboard support systems for the dive.

SERGEI (v.o.)
Does your father know about this?

MARK (v.o.)
He doesn't, and they left Anatoli behind with
the back-up Newtsuit for further lab tests.

The speeding truck suddenly lurches into a tight CURVE in the road.

SERGEI (v.o.)
Oh, my head... take it easy.

INSIDE THE TRUCK CAB

Mark is driving. Sergei is hung-over holding his head in his hands. Kalin, who is sitting between the two men, looks over at Sergei with a sympathetic smile.

KALIN
When was the last time you sat up all
night drinking?

SERGEI
When I got out of the Navy.

MARK
I'd like to hear that story.

KALIN
What part of the service?

SERGEI

Two years out of six working on submarines.
That's when I got interested in underwater
salvage for the navy.

KALIN

So why did you leave?

SERGEI

I couldn't qualify in escape procedures.
My ears wouldn't take the pressure.

Sergei's eyes begin to droop; he's starting to fall asleep. The old truck begins to labor
as it gradually climbs a steep hill.

SERGEI
(groggy)
Just watch your oil pressure...

Sergei slumps back, fast asleep. Kalin looks over at Mark.

KALIN
(concerned)
Does Nikolai know about this trip?

MARK

I told him we were going to visit Anatoli
in St. Petersburg and I'd return in a couple
of days to help him pack his things.

KALIN

You didn't tell him about the dive?

MARK

No, I didn't want him to worry. He's got
enough on his mind right now.

DISSOLVE TO:

HOURS LATER AS HEADLIGHTS PENETRATE A FOG

Sergei's truck slowly crosses the KAZAN BRIDGE to enter the city. The famous silhouette of the onion-domed Church of the Resurrection of Christ appears, and beyond that the magnificent skyline of St. Petersburg.

AT THE KRONSTADT CAR FERRY

the truck glides down a ramp into the morning FOG. Moments later, Gorzenko's Volvo appears and follows the truck. A nearby SIGN on the dockside road reads:

NAKHIMOV NAVAL ACADEMY
3.2 km.

DISSOLVE TO:

AT THE GATES TO THE NAVAL ACADEMY

the truck comes to a stop. A SECURITY GUARD with a flashlight exits his KIOSK and approaches Sergei, who is now driving. He shines his light into the cab.

GUARD
What is your business here?

SERGEI
Lieutenant Tsarkov is expecting us.

The guard looks over at Kalin and Mark, then back to Sergei. He hands Sergei a CLIPBOARD of papers.

GUARD
Everyone must sign their names.

Everyone signs and Sergei hands it back to him.

GUARD
One moment, please.

The guard returns to his kiosk and makes a telephone call, while checking his clipboard. A moment later he steps out and waves them forward.

> GUARD
> Lieutenant Tsarkov is expecting you. He is
> in the last building on the pier marked L-3.

THE SECURITY GUARD

watches the truck disappear into the fog. Moments later, the Volvo stops at the gate. The guard instantly recognizes Gorzenko and salutes him smartly. They exchange information, then he waves him through.

IN THE NAVAL YARD

the truck passes the historic ADMINISTRATION complex and soon comes to a stop in front of a large building marked L-3.

ANATOLI

looks fresh and smart in his immaculate uniform as he steps from the doorway of the building to greet everyone as they step out of the truck.

> ANATOLI
> (to Mark)
> It's great to see you again.

Anatoli looks over at Kalin and they hug.

> ANATOLI
> I'm glad you're helping us.

> MARK
> (to Anatoli)
> This is my friend, Sergei Kozlov.

> ANATOLI
> Mark has told me about you.
> (they shake hands)
> Let's get onboard. Everything is ready
> to go with the Admiral's blessing.

Anatoli's mention of the Admiral stops Mark for the moment.

MARK

The Admiral knows about this?

ANATOLI
(matter-of-fact)
Yes... it was best to get his approval for
this operation, and that's what I did.

MARK
(surprised)
How'd you ever swing that?

ANATOLI
(matter-of-fact)
I told him that there were minor shallow
water dives that had to be conducted before
Doctor Fletcher returned and he agreed.
No one will question my decision.

Sergei looks over at Mark and nods his approval.

SERGEI
(smiles)
I like his style already.

DISSOLVE TO:

EARLY MORNING ON THE SEA

the R.V. ANASTASIA, an ultra-modern 81-ton research vessel with a twin hull, cuts
effortlessly through the water. On the stern deck next to the open diving well is the
back-up YELLOW NEWTSUIT, on a stand. On the portside a ZODIAC rests in a
hydraulic launching frame, with a helicopter PAD aft of the WHEELHOUSE.

INSIDE THE WHEELHOUSE

Anatoli is giving the group a brief tour of the electronic equipment.

ANATOLI
That's our G.P.S., global positioning system.
Gives your location anywhere in the world
within seconds, give or take a few feet.

Anatoli leads them to the other side of the wheelhouse.

> ANATOLI
>
> This is the sub-sea console, with side scan,
> seismic monitor and sub-bottom profiler.
> Everything is multiplexed to the operations
> station on the stern deck when we dive.

> SERGEI
>
> How do you anchor this rig?

> ANATOLI
>
> We don't. We can maintain an exact location
> with the D.P.S. dynamic positioning system,
> which is linked to our G.P.S. In other words,
> we don't require anchors.

> KALIN
>
> I'm very impressed... I had no idea you
> knew all this.

Anatoli beams with pride at Kalin's comment.

> MARK
>
> It's all great, but you need an engineering
> degree to keep everything working right.

Sergei suddenly checks his submariner's pocket watch.

> SERGEI
>
> I don't need an engineering degree to tell
> us that we're almost over our dive site.

Anatoli reacts skeptically to Sergei's method of reckoning with his pocket watch, even
though he may be right. He steps to the console and begins to flip switches. A green
light appears on a MONITOR that traces across the SCREEN.

> ANATOLI
>
> We are still over the drop-off, we should
> see the ridge come up any moment now.

Anatoli readjusts the monitor and points to the flashing impulse.

ANATOLI

That's the one hundred and eighty meter line.
There's the ridge at seventy-three meters and...
there's the wreck hanging the edge.

A PRINTER snaps to life with a pattern that shows the bottom contour at two hundred and forty-feet. A moment later, the sonar MONITOR begins to trace the outline of the sunken freighter.

SERGEI
(delighted)
That's it... you're dead on. That's exactly
the place we want to be.

ANATOLI
It's over a hundred and fifty meters long
and appears to be upright in one piece.

MARK
What's that line running diagonally
under her bow?

ANATOLI
I think it's a shadow from the edge of the
ridge. The bow appears to be resting over
the drop off to the deep.

Anatoli studies the monitor for a moment, then looks over at Mark.

ANATOLI
Do you still want to make this dive?
It could be very dangerous down there.

MARK
(optimistic)
Now more than ever. Let's get suited up!

SERGEI
I'll launch the Zodiac over the side.

Anatoli steps over to the Russian HELMSMAN working the WHEEL.

ANATOLI
Helmsman. We're going to our dynamic
positioning. Set the coordinate to maintain
our station over the dive site, then continue
to monitor the system.

The helmsman turns and salutes. It is the face of GORZENKO.

GORZENKO
Yes, sir... right away!

* * *

*This brings us just a little past the **midpoint** of our film. When everything seems just right for our main characters to finally succeed, we pull the rug out from under them once more, or I should say, our cleverly skillful, and cunning antagonist Gorzenko does the job for us, as so he should.*

And ever since Nikolai was forced to beach his tugboat, we have slowly been climbing, scene by scene, to the top of our roller-coaster ride and we are now about to take our audience on a wild ride into the deep. Who would have ever suspected that we would have our arch villain Gorzenko along with us on this dangerous ride? They now face another unknown factor.

*Our audience knows that Gorzenko is out to destroy their plans at any cost, while our main characters have no idea of what is in store for them. This scenario becomes the second **ticking clock** in our story, this one much deadlier than the first one. This will ultimately shift the direction and the basic needs for survival of our main protagonist. Here is a lesson well learned; never neglect the power of the **villain** in your story. If your hero is strong and confident at what he does, your villain should have the same traits, if not more.*

The greatest conflict in your story will always exist between the villain and your hero. By concentrating on your villain, you'll come to understand his point-of-view, how he thinks and how he hopes to achieve his goals. Gorzenko is onboard and it appears he has everything under control. A disaster is in the making.

* * *

GORZENKO

opens an overhead PANEL and activates a series of switches. The high-pitched SOUNDS of distant motors are heard from below. Sergei suspiciously studies Gorzenko's performance for a moment.

> ANATOLI
> We'll be directing operations from the
> diving console on the stern deck. You
> can transfer calls to us at that station.

> GORZENKO
> Yes, sir.

Gorzenko's dispassionate eyes follow the trio as they exit the wheelhouse.

OUTSIDE THE WHEEL HOUSE

Sergei stops Anatoli in the companionway, looking concerned.

> SERGEI
> (suspicious)
> Can your helmsman be trusted?

Anatoli nods with assurance.

> ANATOLI
> He's here to take orders, that's all.

> SERGEI
> And what does that mean?

> ANATOLI
> When we find the gold, he will be well
> compensated for his work onboard.

ON THE STERN DECK

the sea rises and falls inside the open diving well appropriately named the MOON POOL. The Newtsuit rests on a stand. Mark attaches the compact OXYGEN SPHERES into the upper shell. Sergei and Kalin lay out the wire UMBILICAL. Then they unfold a large rubber LIFT BAG across the portside.

> KALIN
> Where will Mark get the air to fill this?

> SERGEI
> After he hooks on, he will use the air in
> the extra tanks to inflate the bag.

Sergei helps Mark fasten TWO additional scuba BOTTLES to the outside of the suit's streamlined shell casing.

> SERGEI
> Can you really handle this space suit?

> MARK
> I was checked out in the tank at ICOR at
> least a dozen times during routine tests.

> SERGEI
> This is not a routine dive in one of your
> tanks. It's a whole new environment.

> MARK
> That's what makes it interesting.

Sergei lowers the hoisting CABLE from the BOOM. Mark turns a wheel. The suit opens like a clam and he eases into the bottom section off a short ladder. Kalin climbs the ladder to kiss him.

> KALIN
> Please look after yourself.

> MARK
> (holds up the talisman)
> I've got the power of Ulysses, remember?

Mark gives Sergei the thumbs-up sign and he lowers the upper half of the Newtsuit over his head. Mark locks it from inside. Sergei snaps the suit's lifting ring to the cable. The SOUND of Mark's voice is heard over the ship's SPEAKERS.

MARK (v.o.)
Anatoli, I'll start the predive checks.

At the dive control CONSOLE Anatoli slips on a HEADSET.

ANATOLI
I'm online. Let's start.

MARK (v.o.)
PO-2, twenty-one percent. Port side 0-2, four-
thousand. Starboard 0-2, at thirty-nine hundred.
The altimeter is set at sea level. CO-2 scrubber
is on and functioning.

Anatoli looks over the readouts, and then keys his communications.

ANATOLI
Roger, it looks good from here.

INSIDE THE WHEEL HOUSE

Gorzenko stands at a window that overlooks the stern deck watching the activity. The
SOUND of Mark's voice is heard from a SPEAKER in the wheelhouse.

MARK (v.o.)
Umbilical release locked. Ballast weight release
locked. Suit separation emergency release locked.
That's it, Anatoli; let's go for the gold!

Gorzenko steps back to the D.P.S. console and watches as the tiny lights flash.

SERGEI'S (v.o.)
Winch controls... are ready to go.

BESIDE THE MOON POOL

Sergei activates the winch and takes up the slack on the overhead cable. The Newtsuit
swings up and over to the moon pool, ready to drop into the sea.

MARK (v.o.)

All stop! Sergei, check that the extra tanks
are turned on. I'd hate to have all that gold
and no air for the lift bag.

Sergei steps over to the pool and quickly checks the tank VALVES. He is satisfied
and goes back to his station.

SERGEI

Roger, they're turned on. Good luck!

Sergei activates the crane and the Newtsuit slowly descends. Mark's face can be clearly
seen through the acrylic viewing port. He smiles at Kalin. She waves back and in the
next brief moment, the yellow suit disappears into the foaming sea.

THE NEWTSUIT UNDERWATER

as the frothing sea rises over the view port, then all is calm, as the tethered figure
slowly descends into the silent depths.

INSIDE THE WHEEL HOUSE

Gorzenko opens a LOCKER and removes a survival OUTFIT, a KNIFE and an auto-
matic PISTOL. He begins to quickly change out of his naval uniform into the survival
clothing. The SOUND of Mark's communications continues.

MARK (v.o.)

Everything is working fine.

SERGEI (v.o.)

You sound good. Just take it easy.

DISSOLVE TO:

MEANWHILE IN NIKOLAI'S STUDY

he continues to pack his BOOKS and PICTURES, stripped from the walls. The telephone rings. He tries to ignore it but it continues to ring.

NIKOLAI

Allo...

CUT TO:

INSIDE THE WHEEL HOUSE OF THE R.V. NORDENSKIØLD

Fletcher paces with a portable TELEPHONE looking very troubled.

> **FLETCHER**
> Nik, I just got a report from our base in
> Kronstadt, that Mark and Anatoli took a
> navy dive boat.

Fletcher steps away from the console to a side entrance for privacy.

> **FLETCHER**
> (half-whisper)
> They also took the other backup Newtsuit!
> Yes... They left four hours ago. Sergei and
> a woman went with them.

Fletcher shakes his head in dismay at what he needs to reveal.

> **FLETCHER**
> Nik, nobody is suppose to know this.
> We're having problems with our seals
> at the shoulders. They're not reliable.
> (in a secretive tone)
> In our recent tests they were rupturing
> anywhere beyond two hundred feet. It
> appears that we have solved the problem
> on the suit we have here, but the suit that
> Mark has taken is not retrofitted yet.

CUT TO:

NIKOLAI ON THE TELEPHONE

> **NIKOLAI**
> Does Mark know this?

Nikolai shakes his head; he can't believe what he is hearing.

> **NIKOLAI**
> (shocked)
> Nobody does?
> (his face flushes with anger)

Your obsession for winning at all costs may
cost you Mark's life! We need to find him
before it's too late... no... he didn't. He only
said that he was going to see Anatoli for a
couple of days.

Nikolai now notices a PAD beside the telephone with one of Mark's DOODLES drawn
on it and casually picks it up.

>   NIKOLAI
>   That's what I don't understand. Why would
>   they take the Newtsuit with them?

CUT TO:

NIKOLAI'S P.O.V. OF MARK'S DOODLE

of a SHIP outline with the word PRINCE penciled across the bow. A stream of bubbles
containing DOLLAR SIGNS rises from the deck hatches.

>   NIKOLAI (v.o.)
>   Ian, I know exactly where they are.
>   Let me give you their coordinates.

CUT TO:

FLETCHER IN THE WHEEL HOUSE

at a CHART-TABLE as he writes down the site coordinates on the edge of a chart.

>   FLETCHER
>   59.29 North... 23.58 East... yes, I'll be
>   there as soon as the chopper is back.

He folds up the chart, slips it inside his jacket, then checks his watch.

>   FLETCHER
>   I'll try and make radio contact with them,
>   then we'll contact you on your workboat.
>   And Nik... don't worry, Mark is not going
>   to do anything foolish out there!

DISSOLVE TO:

MARK IN THE NEWTSUIT

continues to slowly descend with an expression of sheer fascination on his face. He begins to search the darkening depths with a LIGHT, strapped to his arm.

> MARK (v.o.)
> This is going to be one great ride!

> SERGEI (v.o.)
> Forget about 'the one great ride.' We
> just need you back all in one piece.

AT DIVE CONTROL

the SOUND of all communications continue from the overhead SPEAKERS.

> ANATOLI
> You just passed one-hundred feet and
> everything looks good at this end.

The hollow SOUND of Mark's confident voice replies.

> MARK (v.o.)
> Slacken the winch line; I'm going to take
> control with the thrusters.

> SERGEI
> Roger... it's all yours.

THE NEWTSUIT

thrusters are activated. Mark turns on his two helmet LIGHTS, which illuminate the suit's upper yellow torso. The high-pitched thrusters quickly slow his descent. He appears to hover, in the dark infinity of the sea, like an ASTRONAUT.

GORZENKO IN THE WHEEL HOUSE

is now dressed in his black survival outfit. The SOUND of Mark's voice continues over the speaker. Gorzenko straps a diver's KNIFE to his leg, inserts a CLIP into his handgun and slips it into his HOLSTER.

160

MARK (v.o.)

I've just passed two hundred feet. I'm
going to move forward, I think I'm a
little too far to port for my landing.

Suddenly the SOUND of Fletcher's voice crackles over the ship-to-shore RADIO.

FLETCHER (v.o.)

Fletcher calling the Anastasia do you
read me? Over... calling the Anastasia...
please come in. This is an emergency!

Gorzenko pulls out his knife and immediately cuts the CABLES to the radio.

THE NEWTSUIT

now surges forward as Mark applies full forward power to the thrusters, as he continues
to search the depths with his light.

SERGEI (v.o.)

You should be able to see it any minute.

CUT TO:

MARK'S P.O.V. OF A SHAPE

as the ghostly WRECK appears faint, then more discernible as he comes closer.

MARK (v.o.)
(excited)

I've got the Prince! She's right below me.

SERGEI (v.o.)

Go steady, Mark.

A few snagged fishing NETS drape the encrusted rigging. The wreck's profile looks
like a classic LIBERTY SHIP. Schools of FISH dart in and out of the black tomb-like
OPENINGS, to the cargo holds.

CUT TO:

THE NEWTSUIT

descends closer. He shuts down his thrusters and focuses his light. The tapering BOW
of the old wreck hangs precariously over the edge of the ABYSS.

                              MARK (v.o.)
                 It's all in one piece, and upright!

Mark carefully powers his way around CABLES, hanging from a dismembered cargo
BOOM, and lands on the encrusted stern DECK. His landing erupts a fine orange rust
CLOUD that drifts upward with the current into the black stillness.

                              MARK (v.o.)
                 Touch down! I'm on the port side, near
                 the stern deck. We're right on target!

AT DIVE CONTROL

Sergei, Anatoli and Kalin are elated by Mark's initial success.

                               SERGEI
                 Welcome to The Prince of Russia!

                               KALIN
                 Congratulations, Mark.

                              ANATOLI
                 Great job, Mark!

THE NEWTSUIT

takes a slight spin, as an unseen current suddenly buffets Mark. It forces him to grab
the rusted RAILING near him with a MANIPULATOR, to keep his balance.

                              MARK (v.o.)
                 There's a very strong under current here
                 running along the ridge.

AT DIVE CONTROL

Anatoli flips a switch and takes a reading.

162

ANATOLI
Our monitor reads three knots.

Sergei spreads out an aging DECK PLAN of a similar FREIGHTER.

SERGEI
Try and head inboard. The companionway
should be directly forward from where you
are on the portside... with a stairway.

MARK (v.o.)
I see it... I'm heading in, but I'll have to
drop the thruster pack.

Mark activates the thruster pack release, it drops onto the DECK.

DISSOLVE TO:

NIKOLAI'S OLD WORK BOAT

squats low in the water from the weight of a large COMPRESSOR at the stern. The
diesel screams, under full throttle, as she slides down the oncoming swells in a churn-
ing headway to the open SEA.

INSIDE THE WHEELHOUSE

Nikolai's struggle to keep control of the WHEEL, plus the violent motion of the sea
puts pressure on his fractured ribs. He grits his teeth with the pain. Suddenly, the
SOUND of Fletcher's voice is heard over the ship-to-shore SPEAKER.

FLETCHER (v.o.)
Fletcher calling Nikolai. Hello Nik... can
you read me? Over.

The frequency rattles with offshore chatter.

NIKOLAI
Go ahead Ian, I read you.

CUT TO:

FLETCHER

is standing near the helicopter PAD, on the research vessel, with a phone in his hand.
A SIKORSKY SEA KING is being serviced by a Russian maintenance crew.

> FLETCHER (v.o.)
> Nik, I've alerted the Estonian Coast Guard.
> They're standing by. I've tried to communicate
> with the Anastasia... but they're not receiving.
> We're just about to take off from here, so I'll
> see you on the site. Over and out.

The ENGINES come to life and Fletcher climbs onboard. The rotor BLADES quickly
increase their revolutions and the powerful aircraft lifts off.

> DISSOLVE TO:

INSIDE THE CARGO HOLD

Mark steps off the rusted STAIRCASE. The yellow shafts of LIGHT from his two
helmet lights pierce the darkness in front of him like headlights in a fog.

> MARK (v.o.)
> I'm at two hundred and forty-feet. I've just
> come down one flight of stairs and through
> a hatchway.

> SERGEI (v.o.)
> Keep going, you're in the cargo area.

> CUT TO:

MARK'S P.O.V. OF THE CARGO AREA

He pans his LIGHT along a cluster of violet colored sea URCHINS attached to the
bulkhead. He walks forward into the silent darkness. He now sees row after row of
badly rusted American WW II TANKS. Their sponge encrusted barrels point upwards
and colored SEA FEATHERS sprout from their muted muzzles.

> MARK (v.o.)
> This place looks like a used car lot. The
> hold is full of American tanks!

ANATOLI (v.o.)
Come again?

MARK (v.o.)
Army tanks... I'm looking at a fortune in
scrap metal down here.

SERGEI (v.o.)
You're looking at the wrong fortune.

CUT TO:

DIVE CONTROL

as Sergei continues to check the freighter's DECK PLAN.

SERGEI
Go along the port side as far as you can.
The gold locker has a set of double doors.

IN THE CARGO HOLD

Mark continues along the uneven decking. The wreck unexpectedly shudders in the
strong current. Bits and pieces of jagged metal and debris DRIFT downward in a cloud
of silt. Then the shaking stops as quickly as it started.

MARK
I can feel the current moving the hull.
It's very strong.

SERGEI (v.o.)
If it gets any worse, you're out of there!

MARK
(cocksure)
Not until I find the gold!

Mark's lights illuminate more outcroppings of sea urchins attached to a collection of
rusting OIL DRUMS. Then he sees a set of DOORS that are half open.

MARK
(excited)
I see the doors! They're half open.

165

GORZENKO

lifts an aluminum hard-shell BRIEFCASE out of a nearby locker.

> MARK (v.o.)
> I'm now inside the lock up.

Gorzenko lays the briefcase down, on the chart table, and carefully opens it.

> SERGEI (v.o.)
> According to our research, the chest tops
> are bonded with a gold eagle head!

CUT TO:

GORZENKO'S P.O.V. OF THE BRIEFCASE

that is filled with plastic EXPLOSIVES. He takes a WIRE and connects it to an electronic TIMER that is connected to a sophisticated detonating device.

CUT TO:

GORZENKO

closes the briefcase, satisfied with the connection, and goes back to the helm.

CUT TO:

MARK

clamps his MANIPULATORS onto the doors and pulls them fully open. A large LING COD, just inside the doors, PANICS and shoots straight at Mark's face. Startled by the fish's quick movement he spins and falls against the doors.

> MARK (v.o.)
> God...damn!

> SERGEI (v.o.)
> What's going on? Are you okay?

Clouds of rising silt block out his LIGHT, as Mark regains his balance.

                    SERGEI (v.o.)
                    (concerned)
              Mark, do you read me?

                       MARK
              Yes, I just met the guardian of our gold.

                    ANATOLI (v.o.)
              Come again?

                       MARK
              There's a big fish down here!

MARK

enters the room. Fallen BEAMS hang from the dismembered ceiling above him, which
restrict his movements as he surveys the room. Then he sees four chests.

                       MARK
                 I see four chests in here. And they
                 look to be in good shape.

                                                          CUT TO:

MARK'S P.O.V. OF THE CHESTS

as his LIGHT reveals an American eagle EMBLEM stenciled on the lids.

                    MARK (v.o.)
              There's eagles on the lids!

                                                          CUT TO:

AT DIVE CONTROL

the trio let out a cheer. Sergei gives Anatoli and Kalin a bear hug.

                      SERGEI
                 I knew we could do it!

                      KALIN
              Mark... that's fantastic!

> ANATOLI
> I'm sending down the lift bag on a running
> shackle. It'll take a few minutes.

> MARK (v.o.)
> Roger... I'm going to open the first chest!

MARK

hooks the MANIPULATOR under the corroded lid and lifts. A thick CLOUD of silt
drifts off with the lid being opened, obscuring the contents.

CUT TO:

MARK'S P.O.V. OF THE OPEN CHEST

as the silt settles, the interior now becomes visible. It is EMPTY.

CUT TO:

MARK

swings his manipulator into the empty chest. There is nothing to find.

> MARK
> It's gone. The chest is EMPTY!

> SERGEI (v.o.)
> I can't believe it... are you sure? What
> about the other chests?

Mark stumbles around to the next chest and opens the lid. It is EMPTY. And when he
opens the other two, they are also empty. The gold is missing!

> MARK
> They're all empty, every one! Someone
> got here before us. There's no gold here!

FADE TO:

* * *

*The fact that the gold has been taken is no surprise to our audience. They have
been in on this little secret since Act One, when the Admiral hired Gorzenko to
do his dirty work. It's called* **dramatic irony**. *Now that our heroes have suddenly*

discovered the same secret, it's a major disappointment and a terrible letdown for everyone on the dive.

*It also deepens the tragic financial circumstances for Nikolai and Sergei. We've reached approximately eighty minutes of screen time in our story. We still have Gorzenko to contend with, who is obviously planning to destroy the research vessel and everyone onboard, most likely before the arrival of Nikolai and Fletcher. This further increases the **anxiety** of our audience. It also increases their empathy for Mark and his associates. But time is running out.*

*And our torturous **ticking clock** is still working.*

*   *   *

Act Two – Card #9

GORZENKO IN THE WHEEL HOUSE

carefully folds up his UNIFORM and stows it in the locker. Mark and Sergei's voices continue to be heard over the wheelhouse speaker.

SERGEI (v.o.)
Mark... I'm really sorry, I don't understand.
Nik and I were so sure that the gold would be there.

MARK (v.o.)
(shattered)
I know... we all thought so.

ANATOLI (v.o.)
Let's get you back up here.

MARK (v.o.)
(disappointed)
Okay... take up my slack, Sergei, I'm
on my way!

Gorzenko checks his watch, picks up the aluminum briefcase with his DIVE BAG, and cautiously steps out onto the upper DECK.

DISSOLVE TO:

MARK

turns and slowly works his way back, around the hanging steel beams and the clutter of debris, toward the exit.

DISSOLVE TO:

NIKOLAI

contines to struggle at the helm, as his small workboat surges forward. He scans the horizon with his BINOCULARS in anticipation. Suddenly, he makes out the outline of the Anastasi on the horizon and picks up his ship-to-shore RECEIVER.

NIKOLAI
Nik calling Fletcher. Do you copy? Over.

The frequency is full of static and power lags. Then the SOUND of Fletcher's voice abruptly resonates through the wheelhouse SPEAKER.

INSIDE THE SIKORSKY HELICOPTER

Fletcher rechecks a CHART, and then shows the PILOT the location. He nods his understanding and realigns one of his instruments. The helicopter makes a slight adjustment, banking to the left.

FLETCHER (v.o.)
Hello, Nik... I read you. Over.

NIKOLAI
(matter-of-fact)
I have the Anastasia in sight. I should be
alongside in fifteen minutes. Over.

FLETCHER
Okay Nik, we're right on course. I just hope
we arrive in time. Over and out.

DISSOLVE TO:

AT DIVE CONTROL

Sergei steps to the portside and activates the winch control. The motor starts to slowly retrieve the UMBILICAL out of the moon pool. Anatoli continues to monitor the sub-sea readouts with Kalin.

170

MARK (v.o.)
Hold it, Sergei. I just need a second to
untangle my umbilical.

Kalin points to Mark's readout screen, looking concerned

KALIN
His respiratory rate is rising.

SERGEI
Mark, take it easy. We've got lots of time.

GORZENKO

descends the wheelhouse LADDER with his briefcase and bag to the lower portside.
He comes to the ENGINE ROOM, opens the door and steps inside.

SERGEI AT THE WINCH CONTROLS

happens to look up, just in time to see the engine room DOOR slowly closing. Sergei
does a double take. The door wouldn't close by itself like that.

SERGEI
Anatoli, take over the winch. I'm going
to check on the engine room.

CUT TO:

GORZENKO'S P.O.V. OF THE OPEN BRIEFCASE

as he arms the explosives by switching on the electronic timer. The device begins a
countdown from FIVE MINUTES. He closes the briefcase and locks it.

CUT TO:

GORZENKO IN THE ENGINE ROOM

places the briefcase under the DIESEL. Suddenly a shadow moves across the decking in front of him. Gorzenko looks up just as Sergei steps forward holding a heavy
WRENCH in his hand.

SERGEI
(sees the briefcase)
That's full of explosives!

171

GORZENKO

You're very observant.

SERGEI

(steps closer)

Who are you?

GORZENKO

Just a man on a mission.

Gorzenko draws his pistol. Sergei makes a lunge with the wrench, which knocks the pistol aside, just as the gun fires. The bullet barely misses Sergei. The two men fall back against the diesel in a frenzied life or death struggle.

Gorzenko's ability in a hand-to-hand combat is far superior. He brings up a swift knee into Sergei's stomach, doubling him over, then double chops him across the back of the neck. Sergei collapses onto the floor.

AT DIVE CONTROL

both Kalin and Anatoli hear the SOUND of the gun.

KALIN

What was that?

ANATOLI

I'm going to check.

Anatoli runs toward the engine room. The whining SOUND of the winch motor continues as Kalin checks the read-outs.

AT THE HATCHWAY TO THE ENGINE ROOM

Anatoli is met by Gorzenko. He shoves his gun in Anatoli's face and backs him against the ship's railing. Anatoli is helpless.

GORZENKO

(threatening)

I have no quarrel with you, so stand aside
and stay out of my way.

ANATOLI
Why are you doing this?

Gorzenko drops his dive bag into the ZODIAC that is moored alongside, and then starts to climb over the rail, all the while holding his gun on Anatoli

GORZENKO
I've got little time to explain, but I want
to thank you for the Zodiac!

Anatoli makes a desperate move toward him. Gorzenko smashes him point-blank across the head with the butt of his gun. Anatoli reels with the impact and drops to the deck. Gorzenko holsters his pistol and turns to the rail, ready to climb over.

Sergei suddenly lunges out of the hatchway, with the aluminum BRIEFCASE, and rams it into Gorzenko's back crushing him into the railing. Sergei then makes a powerful swing of the briefcase, aimed squarely at Gorzenko's head, but Gorzenko instantly regains his balance and deflects the briefcase with his elbow.

The briefcase is sent flying into the air and drops into the SEA.

Gorzenko pulls his pistol, but Sergei smashes his hand against the railing and the pistol slides along the deck. Gorzenko staggers Sergei with a quick combination of chops to his head, and then he pulls his KNIFE to finish him off.

Suddenly, a SHOT rings out. Gorzenko is hit in the chest. Looking stunned by the shot, he pushes Sergei aside and proceeds to climb the rail.

Then he painfully turns and instinctively raises his knife to throw it at the person that shot him. Another SHOT rings out and slams into his chest, he teeters on the rail, then falls OVERBOARD. Gorzenko is dead before he hits the water.

SERGEI

staggers to his feet, astounded by the change of events.

CUT TO:

SERGEI'S P.O.V. OF KALIN

who steps forward, holding Gorzenko's smoking gun in her hand.

173

KALIN
He was going to kill you!

AT THE RAIL

Sergei helps Anatoli to his feet and they quickly return to dive control.

ANATOLI
Let's get Mark up and get the hell out
of here as quickly as possible!

MARK ON THE WRECK

has cleared his umbilical and is now situated on the stern DECK. He sights his THRUSTER pack nearby and carefully moves toward it.

THE BRIEFCASE

lands on the starboard side of the deck, unseen by Mark. It bounces along in the swift current, and then slides OVERBOARD into the DEEP.

A split second later, there is a TREMENDOUS EXPLOSION!

THE OLD FREIGHTER'S BOW

pitches forward from the powerful shock wave toward the edge, then eases to a STOP, as a great wall of SAND continues to collapse from the vertical CLIFF.

MARK

is swept off his feet by the impact of the explosion. The DECK pitches violently. SAND and SILT swirl around him. Cables and rigging rain from above. He slides across the deck and slams into the railing, totally out of control.

MARK
(screaming)
Slack off on the umbilical!
Static fills the communications, they can barely hear each other.

SERGEI (v.o.)
Roger... it's done!

174

The rusted railing collapses under his impact and Mark tumbles off the edge of the deck into the dark void beyond.

THE NEWTSUIT

now falls free, as if in slow motion, trailing the TETHER behind. Mark lands on his back onto the sandy SEABED, far below.

MARK

slowly sits up beside the towering FREIGHTER. His communications continue to crackle with static, then total SILENCE. He stands up and tries to regain his sense of direction. He shines his LIGHT into the mysterious darkness.

CUT TO:

MARK'S P.O.V. OF A LARGE DARK SHAPE

as he moves forward searching with his LIGHT. A large turret shape appears in front of him. It's indistinguishable in the swirling SAND. Mark continues to focus on the object, as the sand settles. The beam of light now reveals the conning tower of a SUBMARINE. As he moves closer his light suddenly illuminates a black and white SWASTIKA INSIGNIA, with markings that read: **U-3037**.

CUT TO:

MARK

continues to carefully move forward, overwhelmed by the sight in front of him.

MARK
It's a German U-boat!!!

Mark steps out of the moving sand onto the steel DECKING, almost tripping over two TORPEDOES that are lashed to the deck grating. They appear to be in perfect condition. He continues along the sand-covered bow.

It looks totally intact as he looks down from the RAILING. The shifting SAND continues to uncover more of the sub's superstructure. Suddenly the SOUND of Sergei's voice crackles to life.

SERGEI (v.o.)
Mark! Hello Mark... do you read me?
Over. Hello Mark!

Mark looks around for a moment in amazement, before he answers.

> MARK
> (beyond belief)
> I'm on a German submarine!

AT DIVE CONTROL

All three react in disbelief at the same time.

> SERGEI
> Come again, Mark... Over!

> MARK (v.o.)
> I just found a German U-Boat!

Sergei shakes his head. This doesn't make sense.

> SERGEI
> Are you okay, or did that explosion
> rattle your brain?

> MARK (v.o.)
> I'm fine... but there is a German U-Boat
> down here. I'm standing on the deck!

> CUT TO:

* * *

That is the end of Act Two, and it brings us to our second major **plot point***. It is as though a big hook suddenly dropped out of the sky, just at this point in our story, when all seemed lost. It hooked into our story, thanks in part to our villain Gorzenko and his exploding briefcase, and took us off in a completely different direction. Unbeknown to everyone in our story, including our audience this time, the big hook delivered a German U-Boat!*

It's also called, by the Latin phase, **deus ex machina***. It originated with Greek and Roman Theater, when a stage mechanic would lower actors playing a god or gods on stage to resolve a hopeless situation. The Greek tragedian Euripides is notorious for using this plot device. The first person known to have criticized the device was Aristotle in his Poetics, where he argues that a good tragedy must*

176

remain plausible. If that is the case, I wonder what he would think of some of the films that Hollywood produces these days. In modern terms the deus ex machina has also come to describe an object or an event that suddenly appears and solves a seemingly insoluble problem.

We don't exactly have an insoluble problem, at this point, just another unusual **revelation** to deal with. However, this latest plot twist will surely test both Mark's strengths and especially his weaknesses. With very few choices for him to make under the present circumstances, he must definitely choose the right ones if he hopes to survive.

As we proceed into Act Three we need to bring all of our players to the table. Each one needs to resolve their purpose for being here --- all the loose ends need to be tied together. Traditionally, the third act has more twists and false endings than experienced earlier in the first two acts. Let's see how it works in this story.

*   *   *

ACT THREE – CARD #10 – (the Resolution)

ANATOLI

resets the sub-bottom profiler and checks the images. The sub now shows up.

> ANATOLI
> (composed)
> Can you see any identification marks?

> MARK (v.o.)
> The insignia on the conning tower is U-3037.
> The sub looks in perfect shape. It must have
> been preserved all these years under the sand.

Mark is beside himself with this unimaginable discovery.

> KALIN
> (believes him)
> You really found a U-boat!

MARK (v.o.)
It looks like the sub was pinned under the
freighter's stern. They must have gone down
together to land this way on the bottom.

SERGEI
I wish I were down there with you.

KALIN
Mark... please be careful.

MARK

stops beside the conning tower and looks up. In the BEAM from his light he notices
a deep FURROW along the top section of the disfigured tower.

MARK
It looks like the freighter and the submarine
could have collided, maybe in a fog. There's a
deep crease along the conning tower shroud.
(walks forward)
I'm moving toward the stern deck.

Mark stops beside the stern ESCAPE CHAMBER. He playfully reaches down and tugs
on the release LATCH. To his surprise the hatch springs slightly OPEN.

ANATOLI (v.o.)
Mark, we should get you topside immediately.
That explosion could have damaged your suit.

Mark is captivated that the escape hatch still functions.

MARK
(half-listening)
I just found an open escape hatch!

SERGEI (v.o.)
Mark... give me a break. We're not here to
salvage a U-boat. Anatoli's right. We need
to get you up here as soon as possible.

Mark hooks both MANIPULATORS under the hatch lip and applies full leverage by leaning back, which transfers a lot of pressure on the shoulder seals. The hatch suddenly swings up exposing the dark innards of the U-boat.

MARK

Give me a couple of minutes.

He shines his light inside, fascinated by what he sees, and decides to enter.

MARK

I'm going to disconnect my umbilical,
for a minute. I want to check the inside.

SERGEI (v.o.)

Forget it. It's too dangerous!

MARK

(confident)
I've got plenty of 0-2. I'll switch to backup
communications. I'll be fine. Trust me.

He releases his UMBILICAL and hooks it to the deck GRATING beside the hatch. Then he activates a button on his waist PACK.

MARK

I'm now on backup. Do you read?

SERGEI (v.o.)

Not as well as before... but I can hear you.
And since I'm not down there to stop you,
do me a favor, no longer than three minutes!

MARK

You've got a deal.

With the beam of his HAND LAMP leading the way, Mark drops out of sight into the stern escape chamber.

DISSOLVE TO:

IN THE WHEEL HOUSE

Nikolai swings the wheel and drops back on the throttle, as he quickly guides the old workboat alongside the sleek Anastasia.

ANATOLI

sees him and comes to the RAIL. The boat comes to a STOP and Anatoli secures the lines. Nikolai exits the wheelhouse and Anatoli helps him onboard.

> NIKOLAI
> You must be Anatoli.

> ANATOLI
> And you must be Nikolai.

Anatoli reaches out and they shake hands.

> ANATOLI
> I'm glad to meet you.

> NIKOLAI
> Where's Mark?

> ANATOLI
> He just found a U-boat!

> NIKOLAI
> A U-boat?

Nikolai is both surprised and intrigued by this bizarre information.

> ANATOLI
> An explosion uncovered it from a sandbar
> under the freighter, and it's completely intact.

> NIKOLAI
> An explosion?

Nikolai quickly walks over to the Dive Control Area. Kalin and Sergei continue to monitor the instruments. Nikolai angrily confronts Sergei.

NIKOLAI

What in the hell is going on? I just heard
that Mark is on a submarine! Haul him up!

SERGEI

(surprised to see him)
Nik, we've been trying to get him up.

NIKOLAI

Just haul him up by his tether!

SERGEI

We can't do that.

NIKOLAI

And why not?

ANATOLI

He released it before he boarded the sub.

NIKOLAI

(his face drops)
Now he's inside the submarine?

Sergei tries to clear the static-filled channel, but without success.

SERGEI

We just lost all communications.

NIKOLAI

Sergei, I've got my dive gear onboard. Give
me a hand, I'm going after him right now!

SERGEI

You're not in any condition. Your broken
ribs won't take the pressure to begin with.

NIKOLAI

That doesn't matter. I'm suiting up with or
without your help!

INSIDE THE ESCAPE CHAMBER

the space is large enough for four men, which allows the Newtsuit to comfortably maneuver. Mark pans his light. Pipes, gauges and valves cover the walls and everything appears to be in pristine condition. Then his light reveals a gruesome sight. Holding onto the wall is the stark remains of a SKELETON.

CUT TO:

MARK'S P.O.V. OF THE SKELETON

as he pans his lamp up to the grinning SKULL. The German SAILOR is still wearing the remnants of GOGGLES and a metal escape lung CANISTER around his NECK. His gnarled HAND still clutches the chamber DISCHARGE VALVE.

MARK (v.o.)
I'm in an escape chamber!

CUT TO:

INSIDE THE ESCAPE CHAMBER

Mark reaches up with his manipulator to an overhead VALVE when unexpectedly his arm locks into position. It takes all of his strength to pull it DOWN with his other manipulator. The shoulder SEAL suddenly RUPTURES. A showering spray of freezing SEAWATER immediately enters the suit. Mark panics.

MARK
Sergei... I'm FLOODING!

The communications remain SILENT. Mark's reaction is immediate frenzy as freezing seawater continues to fill the Newtsuit.

MARK
Can anyone hear me???

There is no reply only STATIC. Mark looks at the grinning skeleton then at the skeleton's HAND on the DISCHARGE VALVE. As the water inside his Newtsuit steadily bubbles up around his neck.

Mark grabs the overhead hatch, unhooks the LOCKING-BAR and pulls it down for a seal. He knocks the skeleton's hand aside and twists the discharge valve to OPEN. Mark just manages to gulp the last of the AIR and holds his breath, as the surging water begins to fill his acrylic viewport.

NIKOLAI AND SERGEI

Are now working feverishly with Nikolai's antiquated HARD-HAT GEAR.

NIKOLAI
We're running out of time.

Only the SOUNDS of static and garbled noises are heard over the ship's SPEAKERS as Anatoli and Kalin continue to monitor the equipment.

THE SIKORSKY HELICOPTER

suddenly swoops over the VESSELS in a tight circle, then begins a quick descent towards the Anastasia's LANDING PAD.

CUT TO:

INSIDE THE ESCAPE CHAMBER

Mark is now desperate. He reaches back and activates the small VALVE attached to his auxiliary AIR TANKS. An eruption of high-pressure air explodes into the CHAMBER. The water level begins to drop, as SPRAY flies in all directions leaving behind a fine vapor and a DRY CHAMBER.

Mark is staggering, but manages to lock his good manipulator onto an overhead PIPE while pushing down on the separation LEVER. The Newtsuit bursts OPEN at the waist. The trapped seawater gushes out and Mark gasps for AIR!

THE SIKORSKY HELICOPTER

slowly settles on the pad. Fletcher runs toward the stern deck. The helicopter LIFTS into the sky and heads toward the horizon.

A MOMENT LATER

Fletcher joins Nikolai, as he continues to suit up, beside the moon pool.

FLETCHER
Where's Mark?

NIKOLAI
He's inside a German U-boat.

FLETCHER
He's what!?

NIKOLAI
Mark found a sub and unhooked his umbilical
to look inside. That's all we know.

FLETCHER
Can we still talk to him?

NIKOLAI
I'm afraid not.

Sergei quickly adjusts Nikolai's eighty-pound weight belt.

SERGEI
We lost communications with him.

FLETCHER
What's the depth?

SERGEI
Around two hundred and forty feet.

FLETCHER
Damn it!

Fletcher glances at the vintage copper HELMET, on the deck beside Nikolai.

FLETCHER
You're planning to dive over two hundred
feet in this gear, and with two broken ribs?

Nikolai nods confidently as Sergei continues to lace up one of his twenty-pound
BOOTS. Fletcher grabs the other BOOT and tosses it aside.

FLETCHER
You're not going anywhere in this outfit, Nik!

INSIDE THE ESCAPE CHAMBER

Mark lifts himself out of the flooded bottom of the suit and slides out of the top section, dripping wet. This upper half is left hanging by the one arm from the PIPE. He breathes easier, glad to be alive. The talisman hangs from his neck.

> ### MARK
> Great, it's equalized...

He unlocks the light from his suit and shines it around the chamber. He discovers an ENTRY HATCH in the floor. He kneels down, with his ear to the hatch, and hammers on it. A distinct ECHO is heard from under the hatch.

> ### MARK
> Sounds dry to me.

Mark spins the WHEEL on the hatch, which unlocks it, and swings it OPEN. The upward rush of cold stale AIR is damp and musty. It makes him cough.

He unhooks the two smaller OXYGEN TANKS from his backpack and cracks both valves. A high-pressure blast of OXYGEN ventilates the compartment. With the light in his hand he descends down a LADDER into the dark interior.

> DISSOLVE TO:

AT THE MOON POOL

Fletcher is now dressed in Nikolai's DIVING SUIT. Sergei stands by ready to fit the diving helmet, as Nikolai makes a final adjustment to his weight-belt.

> ### NIKOLAI
> When was the last time you went diving in
> a hard-hat?

> ### FLETCHER
> (matter-of-fact)
> Before Viet Nam... when I was training
> navy divers in Hawaii.

> ### NIKOLAI
> (shakes his head)
> Well this isn't Hawaii, so look after yourself
> down there.

FLETCHER
Let's button her up.

Sergei lowers the brass helmet over his head and locks it in place.

INSIDE THE SUBMARINE

Mark steps off the ladder and pans the space with his light.

CUT TO:

MARK'S P.O.V. OF THE INTERIOR

as the bright light reveals a wall of grease-covered TORPEDOES in long racks. They cover the entire length of the musty compartment. He reaches out and runs his hand along one of the torpedoes.

MARK (v.o.)
It's a damn torpedo room!

CUT TO:

IN THE TORPEDO ROOM

Mark is awed by the destructive power of the EXPLOSIVES around him as he moves along the aisle, shivering with the cold.

MARK
(shouting)
Hello...anyone home?

The SOUND of his voice echoes down the metallic chamber. His light suddenly illuminates a group of SAILORS lying in their BUNKS, under the torpedo racks.

CUT TO:

MARK'S P.O.V. OF THE SAILORS

that are now SKELETONS still dressed in the tattered remains of their uniforms. Empty liquor BOTTLES and the packaged remains of FOOD RATIONS litter the bunks. He turns away from the stark reality of the scene around him.

MARK (v.o.)
Trapped in their own iron coffin!

CUT TO:

MARK

finds a stack of BLANKETS in the rack, and still shivering from the cold, he pulls one down and wraps it around his shoulders, then moves on toward a bulk-head.

FLETCHER AT THE MOON POOL

steps onto a dive PLATFORM equipped with FLOOD LIGHTS and a VIDEO CAMERA. The SOUND of his voice echoes from the speakers.

FLETCHER (v.o.)
Nik, get the decompression chamber ready,
just in case I need it when I get back!

NIKOLAI
We'll be ready for you.

Sergei activates the overhead crane and the platform drops into the sea, slicing through the foamy interface in a wash of bubbles.

THE PLATFORM QUICKLY DESCENDS

below the surface. The color of the sea around Fletcher soon changes from a light blue to a dark indigo. The LIGHTS search below like a tracking SPACESHIP, as a steady stream of bubbles trail from the exhaust valve of his HELMET.

ANATOLI (v.o.)
(to Fletcher)
I put an audio coupler on the platform. We
might be able to talk to Mark inside the sub.

Fletcher scans the depths below as his descent continues at a rapid ear-bursting rate. His mouth forms a series of contorted shapes as he attempts to equalize his ears. Fletcher's VOICE is distorted by the increasing pressure as he goes deeper.

FLETCHER
Roger... I read you, Anatoli.

DIVE CONTROL

as they watch Fletcher's descent on a MONITOR.

                    FLETCHER (v.o.)
          Tell Nik that his helmet smells like a Cuban
          cigar factory!

                    NIKOLAI
                    (smiles)
          You should be so lucky.

Anatoli receives a communiqué on the ship-to-shore FAX.

                    ANATOLI
          I just received a reply from Naval Records.
          The U-3037 was the latest TYPE XXI Class
          U-Boat that was assigned to the 4th Flotilla.
          It went to sea on April 22, 1945 from Bremen
          on a training mission with 57 men onboard.
          Its last report was from Bergen, Norway.

                    NIKOLAI
          That's just when the war ended.

                    SERGEI
          What was it doing here?

                    ANATOLI
          That's what is really strange. They can't find
          any record of it ever being in the Baltic Sea!

                                        DISSOLVE TO:
                         *   *   *

*We now have a mystery submarine that Mark, with all his fearless curiosity, has
boarded, through no fault of his own. If he had been in the open sea, instead of the
U-boat escape chamber, he would certainly have perished when the shoulder seal
ruptured.*

*However, Mark now finds himself in the same position as the crew of the sub, when
a portion of the freighter's hull settled on top of the sub's escape hatch, locking all
onboard the U-boat in an iron grave.*

Our story has also reached a dramatic high for our audience. We have created a
***suspension of disbelief** in their minds. For them, it is most feasible that Mark has*
somehow stumbled onto the U-boat and it is just as natural that he should explore the
interior, without much thought of how he will survive. It is ironic that he sees death
all around him, men who could not escape when the U-boat sunk, yet his curiosity,
at this point, is stronger than his thoughts of survival.

We can only play this element in our story for a very short time. The reality is the
fact that his life is running out the longer he is trapped onboard. An attempt to save
him is on the way, but there are no guarantees that it will be successful.

*   *   *

ACT THREE – CARD #11

INSIDE THE SUBMARINE

Mark enters the CONTROL ROOM and finds a SKELETON sitting at a CHART
TABLE with a pencil clutched between his bony fingers. His light illuminates a
COMMANDER'S HAT and a discolored CHART on the table beside the skeleton.

CUT TO:

MARK'S P.O.V. OF A CHART OF THE BALTIC SEA

with a pencil line drawn from the port of BERGEN, through the Baltic Sea, to the
port of SUNDSVALL, on the North-East coast of SWEDEN.

MARK (v.o.)
They were going to Sweden!

CAMERA WIDENS:

The skeleton appears to be looking at Mark with an inquisitive expression.

CUT TO:

MARK

finds himself curiously interested in this lonely figure that was once in command.

MARK
Sorry you didn't make it ...

189

Mark then sees a SKELETON, sitting in a nearby alcove, wearing the remains of a white dress uniform. His bony fingers are holding empty bottle of CHAMPAGNE.

                              MARK
                     Must've been some party.

He turns away from this gruesome scene. A sudden chill passes through his body. The air is cold and stale, he finds it hardly breathable.

                              MARK
                         (feeling dizzy)
                     I've got to stay alive...

                                                              CUT TO:

FLETCHER ON THE DIVE PLATFORM

is overwhelmed by what he sees as the lights reveal the sight of the freighter and the submarine, far below on the edge of the black ABYSS.

                          FLETCHER (v.o.)
                     I have the wrecks in sight. The freighter is
                     right on the edge of the drop-off with the
                     submarine pinned underneath.

                                                              CUT TO:

FLETCHER'S P.O.V. OF THE DARK DROP-OFF

under the bow of the freighter. It forms a foreboding contrast to the enormous brightly lit sandy slope that the submarine and the wide stern of the freighter rest against. Mark's UMBILICAL sways in the current near the conning tower.

                          FLETCHER (v.o.)
                     No sign of Mark, but I see his umbilical
                     line hooked on the sub.

                                                              CUT TO:

AT DIVE CONTROL

they see the images from the camera on the platform, for the first time, and are amazed how precariously the vessels are perched on the very edge of the abyss.

190

ANATOLI
This doesn't look good.

FLETCHER (v.o.)
Slow my descent.

NIKOLAI
Roger.

A SEISMIC SCREEN sparks to life. The reference line begins to jump. Kalin tries to read the printout, and then turns to Anatoli for help.

KALIN
What is your reading of this?

ANATOLI
It looks like the face of the drop-off is continuing
to collapse under the vessel's weight.

SERGEI
Must've been fractured by the explosion.

INSIDE THE SUBMARINE

as it violently pitches and rolls. Mark is thrown off his feet and hurled across the control room floor. He is showered by flying debris and lands shaken and dazed on his back. His light goes out leaving the compartment in blackness.

MARK
(groggy)
What's happening?

Mark slowly regains his senses and flips on the light. The beam reveals a withered SKULL, resting inches from his face. It stares back in ghastly silence.

MEANWHILE AT DIVE CONTROL

they watch the monitor in horror as the sandy RIDGE around the wrecks starts to shift. Plumes of silt are caught in the swirling current as a wall of SAND cascades over the edge into the deep. The wrecks slowly shift position, closer to the EDGE.

ANATOLI
The sand keeps shifting over the edge.

SERGEI
We could lose both vessels at this rate.

NIKOLAI
Not before we get Mark out of the U-boat!

FLETCHER ON THE PLATFORM

comes to a stop some twenty-feet above the deck of the submarine.

FLETCHER (v.o.)
Mark's umbilical is beside an entry hatch.
I can make it myself to the deck from here.

ANATOLI (v.o.)
Doctor Fletcher, be aware that the entire
area around the wreck is continuing to shift.

There is no answer from Fletcher as he takes a loop of air-hose and steps off the plat-form. He drifts downward, past the conning tower, and lands on the deck.

FLETCHER (v.o.)
I'm on the deck.

Fletcher follows Mark's umbilical over to the escape hatch. He tries desperately to unlock it, but without success. It is locked from the inside.

FLETCHER (v.o.)
Mark's inside. The hatch is either jammed
or locked from the inside. I can't get in!

INSIDE THE SUBMARINE

Mark is now sitting on the floor with his head in his hands. He notices the amber talisman hanging from his neck and holds the glowing amber up his light.

MARK
(despondent)
Ulysses... where are you?

FLETCHER

pulls a PRY-BAR from his tool kit and gets down on his knees.

> FLETCHER (v.o.)
> Let's see if this works.

Fletcher hammers on the hatch. Then he lowers his helmet and listens.

INSIDE THE SUBMARINE

Mark hears the reverberating SOUNDS on the hull and looks up.

> MARK
> I don't believe it.

He struggles to his feet with renewed energy. He finds a FIRE EXTINGUISHER and hammers the bulkhead two times, only to hear three distinct taps echo back.

> MARK
> Somebody's really out there!

FLETCHER AT THE ESCAPE HATCH

Sits up with a broad smile on his face.

> FLETCHER
> Mark's alive inside the sub. I can hear
> him tapping to my signals!

> NIKOLAI (v.o.)
> Are you sure?

> FLETCHER
> Yes, they're very clear.
> (takes a beat)
> Nik, I need a cutting torch right away!

AT DIVE CONTROL

Nikolai shakes his head. The torch is not the answer.

NIKOLAI
We don't have time. You're already into
a long decompression and the sand slides
are getting worse under the wrecks.

FLETCHER (v.o.)
What're you talking about? Just send me
me down a torch!

An idea suddenly sweeps across Nikolai's face, and he turns to Sergei.

NIKOLAI
Air... Sergei, what we need is AIR!

SERGEI
Air for what?

NIKOLAI
(convinced)
If we can't get Mark out of the sub, we'll
bring the submarine to us!

FLETCHER (v.o.)
(frustrated)
What're you talking about, Nik?

SERGEI
(suddenly realizing)
Nik's right. We just blow the ballast!

NIKOLAI
Isn't that how a submarine works?

SERGEI
You're damn right.

FLETCHER (v.o.)
Nik, what's going on?

NIKOLAI
I'll let Sergei explain.

Nikolai boards his workboat and starts the AIR-COMPRESSOR. Kalin helps him run the AIR-HOSE back to the moon pool, ready to drop overboard.

> SERGEI
> World War II subs had external pressurized
> couplings on their ballast tanks for emergency
> salvage purposes. On U-boats it was located at
> the bow, just behind the anchor hatch.

FLETCHER ON THE SUBMARINE

turns toward the bow as Sergei continues the procedure.

> SERGEI (v.o.)
> We're sending down an air-hose. If the
> hull is still intact it's more than likely that
> the ballast tanks are still operational.

> FLETCHER
> I just hope you're right.

> NIKOLAI (v.o.)
> It's our best plan to save Mark.

> FLETCHER
> (agreeing)
> Then let's try it!

IN THE CONTROL ROOM

Mark listens for any further SOUNDS. The air is getting worse. He begins to cough uncontrollably, barely able to catch his breath. The cold stale air makes him hyperventilate.

CUT TO:

MARK'S P.O.V. OF THE COMPARTMENT

which begins to swim in front of his eyes as he staggers along the bulkhead with no sense of direction. He reaches out to a PIPE on the bulkhead to steady himself but lack of oxygen slows his response, he misses it and falls into the wall.

MARK (v.o.)
What's happening to me?

CUT TO:

MEANWHILE AT THE BOW OF THE SUBMARINE

Fletcher struggles with the air-hose in the ballast tank FITTING. Finally, he makes the connection and opens the VALVE.

FLETCHER
I'm tied in, it's all yours!

ANATOLI (v.o.)
Roger... we read you.

A moment later, air explodes into the sub's ballast tanks. But without warning, the SIDE VENTS erupt with a continuous cloud of ESCAPING air-bubbles.

FLETCHER
(shouting)
We're losing it! It's bypassing the tanks.

SERGEI (v.o.)
(guessing)
The bypass valve must still be open from its last dive, that's the only answer.

FLETCHER
How do we close it?

SERGEI (v.o.)
It closes from the inside.

FLETCHER
(surprised)
Inside the sub?

SERGEI (v.o.)
(matter-of-fact)
There's a ballast lever located at the diving station in the control room.

NIKOLAI (v.o.)
Mark will have to close it.

FLETCHER
How is that possible?

ANATOLI (v.o.)
Mount the audio coupler on the hull, he
may be able to hear us.

INSIDE THE SUBMARINE

the SOUND of escaping AIR is a new experience for Mark. It shocks him back to
reality. Suddenly, Mark hears the distant SOUND of Sergei's echoing VOICE.

SERGEI (v.o.)
Mark, if you read me tap twice.

He can't believe he's hearing the SOUND of Sergei's voice and he stands up.

MARK
Sergei?

Mark slams the fire extinguisher against the hull twice.

SERGEI (v.o.)
In the control room find the diving
wheel on the portside.

He shines the light along the control room wall and finds the DIVING WHEEL. and
slams the fire-extinguisher twice to signal Sergei.

SERGEI (v.o.)
Okay. There is a green ballast lever to the
left of the wheel. Pull it down... all the way!

Mark supports himself against the diving WHEEL and struggles with the LEVER. It
is frozen with age. Weak from lack of oxygen, he tries pulling with all his strength.
But it does not move, it remains LOCKED.

MARK
I can't do it!

197

He falls to his knees, weak and in total despair.

                    SERGEI (v.o.)
              Mark, have you found it?

Mark only looks up in a daze, not sure what is happening.

                    SERGEI (v.o.)
              This is a race for your life! You have to
              do it... Mark, you can do it!

He swings the fire extinguisher against the lever in desperation, then pulls on it with all his strength. Unexpectedly the lever breaks loose and drops into position.

                    MARK
                  (shouting)
         I got it!

The exhilarating SOUNDS of air are immediately heard hammering and rattling into the tanks. Mark's face lights up at the distinct SOUND of Nikolai's VOICE.

                    NIKOLAI (v.o.)
              That's it! You're on your way!

                    SERGEI (v.o.)
              Great job, Mark!

FLETCHER

looks at the vents as the last of the air bubbles stop. The U-boat now takes on a different SOUND as the sub begins to creak and groan with a life of its own.

                    FLETCHER
              It's working... we've got Mark!

                    NIKOLAI (v.o.)
                  (to Fletcher)
              It's not over yet. Once you're back on the
              platform your first decompression stop will
              be at twelve meters. Do you read me?

FLETCHER
Okay at twelve meters!

THE SUBMARINE

is revitalized with the inrushing air and it shows signs of becoming BUOYANT as layers of sand on the deck shift and spill into the swirling current.

INSIDE THE SUBMARINE

Mark is exhausted and short of breath. Suddenly an overhead water pipe bursts. Mark flounders in the cold cascading seawater.

AT DIVE CONTROL

they watch on the camera monitor as the sub begins to shift, then with a slight rise a few feet at the stern. Fletcher can be seen on the forward bow.

SERGEI
She'll be on her way any minute.

The seismic monitor begins to jump again.

ANATOLI
The entire ridge is collapsing!

FLETCHER (v.o.)
This is crazy down here, Nik!

The SOUND of Fletcher's voice is drowned out with static.

NIKOLAI
Fletcher! Get out of there!

THE SUBMARINE

is now angled up at the stern pitching and rolling as a gigantic wall of SAND collapses underneath the sub and cascades over the ridge into the dark abyss.

THE DIVE PLATFORM

Now hangs some thirty-feet above the wrecks with the powerful LIGHTS flooding the rapidly changing scene below.

FLETCHER

is suddenly thrown backwards off his feet as the rising U-boat violently rolls in response to the elements.

THE FREIGHTER

slips toward the edge of the drop-off, as debris and cables tangle with the sub.

A TOW CABLE

attached to the freighter suddenly snags across the sub's superstructure and stretches taut. Fletcher sees it but before he can clear his umbilical the cable slices through his AIR HOSE. Air bubbles explode from the SEVERED END of the umbilical, as it wildly writhes across the shifting deck of the U-boat.

FLETCHER

is thrown hard against the conning tower and collapses.

* * *

Mark has to call upon all of his reserves of strength in an excruciating situation to open the valve. And while we are in the process of saving Mark's life, his father's life is now threatened and possibly lost in his attempt to save his son.

*Our **subplot** of Mark's relationship to his father now meshes with our main **theme** of survival at sea. Our story also takes on a new dimension with the trapped U-boat now released and heading for the surface with Mark onboard.*

In the next ten minutes or so that it takes to reach the end of our story, we want to introduce a few more dramatic twists and turns and revelations that need to be revealed. Keeping the pace that we have established at the beginning of this act is important. It is also most important to fulfill all of our storytelling requirements toward a satisfying and memorable ending for our audience.

* * *

THE PRINCE OF RUSSIA

continues to slip forward in an avalanche of sand and silt, then slides off the ridge into the DEEP. The sub continues to float upwards, clear of all cables and debris.

INSIDE THE SUBMARINE

Mark struggles to his feet in a torrent of spraying seawater and staggers along the swaying compartment with his light. His spirits are renewed. He now enters, half-blind, a HATCHWAY and find himself in a large WARD ROOM. It appears to be filled with rows of stacked metal TRUNKS and wooden BOXES.

The U-boat suddenly bucks. Mark falls back and lands among a collection of FURNITURE. As he rises to his feet, his light illuminates a very macabre scene.

CUT TO:

MARK'S P.O.V. OF A GROUP OF SKELETONS

that are sitting at a round ornate table. A collection of AMBER jewelry hangs from the rotting remains of their uniforms. One sailor wears a moldy fez covered in fine AMBER ornaments that sparkle like new in Mark's bright light.

On the table are the remains of a POKER GAME. Stacks of priceless AMBER are scattered among the dust-covered playing cards in front of each of the skeletons.

> MARK (v.o.)
> They were gambling with millions of
> dollars worth of amber.

CUT TO:

MARK

almost trips over an open CHEST full of priceless AMBER, strewn around the table. A skeleton with a faded S.S. INSIGNIA on the sleeve of his uniform is sitting in a large ornate chair that is delicately fashioned out of AMBER.

CUT TO:

MARK'S P.O.V. OF THE CHAIRS

around the table, as his light reveals the embroidered ROYAL COAT-OF-ARMS of Tzar Peter the Great emblazoned on the amber panel of all the chair backs.

MARK (v.o.)
Tzar Peter the Great...

CUT TO:

AT DIVE CONTROL

they watch the monitor in horror as Fletcher disappears into the swirling clouds of SILT and SAND. Then the great gray shape of the U-3037 fills the screen, on its way to the surface.

NIKOLAI
Pull the platform before it fouls!

ANATOLI
It's already on its way!

THE SUBMARINE

continues an accelerating rise in a vibrant shroud of bursting bubbles. Cables and hoses trail as the sixteen hundred ton sub ascends toward the sun-filled SURFACE.

THE SEA BESIDE THE ANASTASIA

as Nikolai, Sergei, Kalin and Anatoli step to the rail. Faint at first but growing larger, a long cigar-shaped mass appears below, as bubbles begin boil the sea around the *Anastasia*.

Suddenly, a huge blister of cascading water erupts as the pointed BOW of the submarine breaks skyward, breaching half her length before dropping back onto the surface of the sea.

A MOMENT LATER THE ZODIAC

with Nikolai, Sergei and Kalin onboard are alongside the U-boat and quickly scramble onto the draining deck.

ON THE FORWARD DECK OF THE SUBMARINE

Nikolai and Sergei find Fletcher with his severed umbilical-line tangled around the spare torpedoes. They remove his HELMET only to find him pale and lifeless.

202

SERGEI
There was still air in the helmet!

Nikolai quickly massages Fletcher's neck, trying to revive him.

NIKOLAI
He's still breathing.

Fletcher's eyes open and he slowly focuses on Nikolai.

FLETCHER
(in a half whisper)
Where's Mark?

Sergei and Nikolai help him to his feet and quickly walk him toward the zodiac.

NIKOLAI
Mark is safe and you're on your way to
the decompression chamber.

KALIN

climbs the conning tower LADDER and tries to open a HATCH, but she can't budge
it. She turns away to find a second HATCH. Tears fill her eyes as she tries to turn
the auxiliary release WHEEL.

Unseen by Kalin, the wheel begins to slowly turn on the first hatch. It opens and
Mark climbs out into the afternoon sunlight looking exhausted but undaunted. Kalin
falls into his arms.

KALIN
Thank God... you're alive!

Kalin is overcome with emotion as they kiss tenderly. Nikolai appears and joins them.
Mark hugs his grandfather. There are no words spoken, just tears of joy.

DISSOLVE TO:

SOMETIME LATER ON THE ANASTASIA

Mark walks over to the decompression CHAMBER and looks in the VIEW PORT.
Fletcher looks up at him through the glass. Mark hears his father's voice over the
intercom SPEAKER, just above him.

203

FLETCHER
How are you, son?

Mark smiles, glad to see his father alive and well.

MARK
Nik tells me that you saved my life.
I want to thank you...

FLETCHER
I did what I had to.

MARK
I'm just glad you're alive.

FLETCHER
We're both very lucky.

MARK
(nods slowly)
We're lucky to have each other.

Mark reaches out and they join PALMS pressed against the view port. Fletcher smiles easily, for the first time in a long while.

MARK
I'll be here for you, dad.

FLETCHER
That makes it all worthwhile.

DISSOLVE TO:

INSIDE THE WARDROOM OF THE U-BOAT

the loading HATCHES overhead are now open. A brilliant shaft of SUNLIGHT floods the interior. We hear the SOUND of footsteps. The silhouette figures of Mark and Kalin appear and he helps her down a LADDER into the space.

KALIN
Why are we doing this?

MARK
Just close your eyes, you'll see.

Mark helps her off the ladder and he turns her around.

MARK
Okay, now you can open them.

KALIN OPENS HER EYES

and her face registers immediate SHOCK and ASTONISHMENT.

CUT TO:

KALIN'S P.O.V. OF THE AMBER TREASURE

spilling out of wooden BOXES and metal CHESTS. Magnificent decorations of amber
jewelry and amber furniture of all descriptions sparkle in the dazzling mist-filled
SUNLIGHT. A large amber table bears the ROYAL COAT-OF-ARMS of the Tzar.

KALIN (v.o.)
(amazed)
You found the Tzar's lost treasure!

CUT TO:

IN THE WARDROOM

Kalin walks forward into the center of the priceless treasure trove. She is overwhelmed
and without a word they embrace.

DISSOLVE TO:

LATER IN THE ANASTASIA WHEEL HOUSE

Sergei is meeting with Anatoli and Nikolai, as Mark and Kalin enter. Sergei is holding
Gorzenko's DIVE BAG in his hand.

ANATOLI
Mark, we found something that I think
will certainly interest you.
(hands him a photograph)
Our helmsman had this in his dive bag.
Do you recognize it?

MARK'S P.O.V. OF THE PHOTOGRAPH

that Gorzenko had at the railroad station to recognize Mark.

> MARK (v.o.)
> This was taken on the airplane at the
> Admiral's request, you remember that?

INSIDE THE WHEEL HOUSE

Mark shakes his head in disbelief and hands it back to Sergei.

> MARK
> (matter-of-fact)
> That's how Gorzenko was able to recognize
> me at the train station and follow us.

> SERGEI
> It was the Admiral that gave me his
> blessing, when I asked for the dive boat,
> then set-up Gorzenko to finish us off.

> KALIN
> Why would he do such a thing?

> SERGEI
> To cover up the fact that he took the
> Republic's gold with his naval buddies
> during the war. Then he made sure
> that the records were destroyed.

> MARK
> Can we prove that?

Anatoli holds up a small NOTEBOOK and hands it to Mark to look at.

> ANATOLI
> I believe so. We found this in Gorzenko's
> dive bag. It's a day by day report for the

Admiral, along with the money he was
paid for the job. It has the Admiral's private
phone numbers on the front page and details
of every move he made for him.

                    NIKOLAI
                (matter-of-fact)
        It was Gorzenko who slugged you that
        night after he sabotaged the Baltic Star.

                    SERGEI
        The Admiral set this whole thing up, right
        from the very beginning when he learned
        that we were going to dive on the Prince.

                    KALIN
        And he almost got away with it.

Mark looks over at Anatoli and Sergei with the realization that he is lucky to be alive.
The SOUND of a HELICOPTER is heard. Anatoli leaves the wheelhouse and steps
outside onto the deck.

THE SIKORSKY HELICOPTER

descends onto the LANDING PAD. The engines shut down and the Admiral appears,
looking immaculate in his white DRESS UNIFORM. A PILOT with an UZI follows
him. They walk across the deck toward the lone figure of Anatoli.

THE ADMIRAL

stops in front of the young Lieutenant, who does not respond with the customary salute.
The Admiral ignores his response.

                    ADMIRAL
        As your commanding officer I'm here to take
        charge of this vessel. I hold all onboard guilty
        of trying to jeopardize a military operation.

                    ANATOLI
        This isn't going to work, Admiral.

On the Admiral's signal the pilot levers his uzi at Anatoli.

ADMIRAL
Then you're under arrest, Lieutenant.

NIKOLAI (v.o.)
Not in this country, he isn't!

The Admiral turns to see Nikolai and Mark walking toward him.

NIKOLAI
You're no longer in Russia, Admiral. We
happen to be in Estonian waters.

ADMIRAL
(ignores him)
You're all under arrest!

They stop in front of the Admiral. The pilot looks nervous and readies his uzi.

MARK
You tried to kill all of us.

ADMIRAL
I don't know what you're talking about
and I don't really care.

NIKOLAI
Your assassin is dead. We have his notebook
and the photograph that you gave him. That's
really enough evidence to make you care.

The Admiral looks over at Anatoli, who nods in agreement.

ANATOLI
Gorzenko is dead and we know why.
(testing him)
It was you that took the gold shipment
off the Prince of Russia, then destroyed
all the records at the naval bureau.

The Admiral's face flushes in anger and he turns to the pilot.

ADMIRAL
(screaming)
Shoot them... shoot them all!
(the pilot hesitates)
That's an order, Captain. Kill them!

Anatoli tackles the pilot just as the uzi is FIRED. The burst goes high into the air as they wrestle each other to the deck. The Admiral tries to kick Anatoli but Nikolai hits him with a powerful UPPERCUT that floors him. The pilot throws Anatoli aside and leaps to his feet, still holding the uzi.

SERGEI

appears from behind the pilot and pushes Gorzenko's pistol into his ribs.

SERGEI
Freeze... or you're dead.

Anatoli grabs the Uzi from the pilot. Kalin now joins the group. The Admiral staggers to feet as Nikolai gets ready to hit him again, but the Admiral backs off, holding his bruised jaw.

ADMIRAL
Don't be fools! There's enough money for
all of us to buy our financial freedom. You
can have anything you want.

The old Admiral suddenly stops talking and looks around. The faces are void of sympathy. Nikolai shakes his head sadly.

NIKOLAI
We've got our freedom, Admiral. Something
that you won't have for a long while.

DISSOLVE TO:

SOMETIME LATER THIS STRANGE ARMADA

of vessels appears off the COASTLINE with the Anastassia in the lead with Anatoli at the helm, with Fletcher, Mark and Kalin. A short distance behind, Nikolai's workboat has the sub in tow, as a gentle sea rolls over her gray hull.

INSIDE THE WHEELHOUSE NIKOLAI AND SERGEI

are enjoying themselves, each proudly smoking a HAVANA CIGAR. Their ship-to-shore RADIO crackles with the NEWS of the discovery.

> ANNOUNCER (v.o.)
> A German submarine has been found off our
> coastline, filled with the priceless treasures
> of Tzar Peter the Great. We'll bring you
> further reports as this amazing story unfolds...

Sergei snaps off the radio and helps Nikolai relight his cigar.

> SERGEI
> By the way, I didn't know you could
> throw a punch like that... you almost
> broke the Admiral's jaw.

Nikolai smiles as he draws on his cigar.

> NIKOLAI
> (matter-of-fact)
> That was for stealing our gold.

FOUR ESTONIAN MILITARY JETS (STOCK)

suddenly scream out of the crimson sky and circle the sub. They perform a victory salute by dipping their wings, before they disappear into the setting sun.

MARK AND KALIN

are now standing on the bow of the Anastasia as a flotilla of small BOATS and pleasure CRAFTS converge on them, all blowing their horns in celebration.

> KALIN
> How does it feel knowing that you found
> Tzar Peter the Great's lost treasure?

The SOUNDS of marine HORNS and BELLS continue to fill the air around them. Kalin catches his eye and Mark reacts with a broad smile.

210

MARK

I think I like it...

DISSOLVE TO:

THE BALTIC SEA

as the menacing silhouette of the U-3037 cuts through the reflections of a Baltic
SUNSET as it did on a similar summer evening sixty-two years earlier.

SLOW FADE OUT.

* * * **THE END** * * *

*This final act just about wrote itself. Once the research and all the information for
the technical equipment was established, along with the focus of our players, the
scenes came together very quickly. Our characters were on their own.*

*There was no reason to have a long resolution, which would continue on and on, once
we reached the climax in our story. It's obvious for me that the end of our story is
when the submarine surfaces, with Mark and his father still alive. The Tzar's amber
collection is an unexpected bonus for Nikolai's retirement.*

*Originally, the final scene with the Admiral arriving onboard the dive boat was
planned for another day --- the authorities were going to walk into his office and
arrest him. That would have ended our momentum. So to keep things moving, and
to add another twist to the ending, I decided that he should arrive on the heels of
Mark being rescued and challenge them with his military authority. It also takes up
the story while still at sea, and makes for a stronger visual ending – that develops
into the start of a grand celebration, especially with all the boats welcoming our
heroes into port with horns and sirens.*

Hopefully, our audience will feel the same way.

PART FOUR

THROUGH THE STUDY OF TECHNIQUE --- NOT CANOEING
OR LOGGING OR SLINGING HASH --- ONE LEARNS THE BEST,
MOST EFFICIENT WAYS OF MAKING CHARACTERS COME ALIVE,
LEARNS TO KNOW THE DIFFERENCE BETWEEN EMOTION
AND SENTIMENTALITY, LEARNS TO DISCERN,
IN THE PLANNING STAGES, THE DIFFERENCE BETWEEN THE BETTER
DRAMATIC ACTION AND THE WORSE. IT IS THIS KIND OF KNOWLEDGE
THAT LEADS TO MASTERY. MASTERY IS NOT SOMETHING THAT
STRIKES IN AN INSTANT, LIKE A THUNDERBOLT, BUT A GATHERING
POWER THAT MOVES THROUGH TIME, LIKE WEATHER.

JOHN GARDNER

Whenever a producer, a studio executive, or even an agent receives a screenplay, usually from an unknown writer, or to save time with an established writer, the screenplay will eventually end up in a reader's hands. Movie studios and production companies receive tens of thousands of screenplays each year, and executives cannot read them all. So the film industry uses readers to sift through the screenplays in search of those stories that measure up to their standards of writing and many of the other elements they're specifically looking for.

That person will quickly condense your three acts usually into three pages or more by retelling your basic story. He or she will also conclude the report with comments and recommendations. Based on that report the script is passed forward for a possible development deal, or sent back to the writer, or his agent, with the appropriate notes. This report will open the doors for you with a well-written screenplay, or will quickly close them on an ill-conceived story, or just bad writing itself. First-rate storytelling is a scarce commodity these days.

To give you some idea of that process I've included the following reader's report from the Michael Mann Agency written by Tiffany Borders, who is one of the best readers in Hollywood. This original report was based on the screenplay you have just read, describing the story with final comments and recommendations. Since you have already read the screenplay, we can go directly to her final comments.

Note what is interesting to Tiffany and how she interprets the screenplay. Also remember that most readers are looking at a screenplay with certain actors in mind. That includes the production values in your story that will complement the current market place. Popular movie themes have many incarnations.

* * *

THE PRINCE OF RUSSIA

TITLE:	The Prince of Russia
GENRE:	Action/Adventure
SCRIPT BY:	Jack W. McAdam
REVIEWED:	11/15/06
CONCEPT:	Deep-sea diver Mark searches for the supposed treasure-filled wreck of the freighter Prince of Russia, despite the machinations of the Russian military and Fletcher, his own researcher father.

* * *

COMMENTS

This screenwriter continues to show an expert talent for evoking a sense of place. Whether underwater, creeping through the rusting hulls of forgotten ships, or above ground striding the corridors and marine workshops of ICOR, the reader is very much in the scene. This should make coming to a unified vision of the project between producers/directors/actors/cinematographers very simple indeed. It is all on the page in this particular screenplay.

Locations are used well -- the summer palace of Tzar Peter the Great in particular is a memorable scene, especially the grand ballroom. Locations are cleverly used to provide expositions about the past (such as the missing amber treasure) but also to invoke a sense of lasting importance for the events at hand. Handled well, even a small budget could make use of natural screen resonance of such historically significant backdrops.

The writer makes the effort to combine character and place smoothly within scenes -- for example, Nikolai is seen as experienced, aware and poetic when he observes that June is his favorite time of the year because in the air you can smell: "fisherman are burning alder wood to cure the herring." It says a lot about the man and the place where he lives.

Although written supposedly for an eighteen-year old to play Mark, the role could actually be for any age up to the mid-thirties and still work realistically. This widens the band of talent available and allows for drawing actors in their mid-twenties trying to make it into the big leagues without being forgotten (the Andrew McCarthy syndrome). It also gives you the option of Ben Affleck and Brad Pitt types to do an action movie with much more substance than your average blow-em-up one-dimensional hero pictures. A romantic or comic young male actor could really prove his dramatic chops here.

By not focusing on the teen element, Fletcher's age range also widens to allow for older actors wanting to show they can still pull off an action piece without actually having to undergo too much physical strain. However, this is a script with little sex or violence and little vulgarity, so if a teen picture meets somebody's needs there is no harm with sticking to how it is written.

There is only one real female role in the film (Kalin) but if Mark, Anatoli and some of the other handsome hard bodied male divers spend enough time stripping out of wetsuits, a female audience should be satisfied. The true strong female roles here are the sea and the ships: they are the true love interests, claiming the hearts and dreams of each of our leading men.

Fletcher, his wife taken from him by the jealous sea, is obsessed with finding a way to protect men from it. Mark and Nikolai, losing mother and daughter respectively to the sea cannot help but search its depths to find things which have been abandoned. Even Admiral Kochinko has his relationship with the sea, having used her and abandoned her; he fears the secrets she will divulge to the next man who explores the treasures she keeps will incriminate him. Having such a powerfully affecting common element in their lives gives much energy to the conflict between the male leads in this film.

In many bad action films, the villain tells the hero that the two of them are 'very much the same'. Not here. In this film the heroes (Mark and to a lesser degree, Nikolai) and the villains (Admiral Kochinko, and to a much lesser degree, Fletcher) all have the same character qualities: ambition, a tendency to reach further than allowed, self-confidence, anger, and of course the incessant draw of the sea. To have men of such drive go up against each other makes for suspenseful filmmaking at its best.

These characters are made to seem stronger and therefore their battles mightier and big screen-worthy by the well-executed action scenes which build nicely toward the final climax. Each is given moments of power as well as moments of testing so that we see their strengths and courage. We also see what each is willing to sacrifice in order to have what they want from the sea. An issue here is Fletcher's seeming willingness to let a diver die because the diving suit isn't ready for a deep dive just so he can obtain the Russian contract. It is unclear if he will go through with the deal even if he is unable to fix the problem in time, and such confusion renders him untrustworthy, until he redeems himself, puts the Russian deal on hold to save his son's life.

As a villain the Admiral works well, since most of his villainy was half a century ago and the impact of one shipment of gold would be a major difference to anyone were it not for political embarrassment and an unforgiving disgrace to his distinguished military career. This means his issue is all about Old Guilt, mirroring Mark and Fletcher's old guilt issues about the tragic death of Mark's mother. This screenplay moves at a very nice pace, with believable action and character-consistent dialogue. It could probably be made in Canada or Prague with stock Soviet exteriors. It could also be bumped up a notch with the romance, but again, the screenplay works very well as it is, and most likely would reach a larger audience in the end.

RECOMMENDATIONS

When you consider the film *U-571* that made money and simultaneously pulled in good reviews, and *The Perfect Storm*, which was an immediate hit at the box office, this seems like an ideal opportunity to pitch a movie like "The Prince of Russia." It has elements of both films but with a mini-mystery a la the Jack Ryan flicks to boot. Attach a star as Mark or Fletcher or a reputable action director with a studio deal, and this particular film is easily made without much fuss.

EPILOGUE

How do you complete your vision as a storyteller? First of all, you need to bring together a combination of skills as a storyteller. You need to be inspired by an original idea that you feel is unique and creative. You need a story that will appeal to your audience with role models of courage and greatness.

Along with this, you need to write on a daily basis. Explore your characters, know how to structure a story around each one of them and bring them to life. You choose the time. You can work with them early in morning or in the evening. Once you have created the basic framework of your story they will always be there, waiting for you to further define their roles, happy to work with you.

The basic specifics of the challenge each of your characters has to face may differ, but the underlying fundamentals of life, birth, death, loss, and success will never change in our society. What does change, however, is how the audience learns to see and value these events, and that's our job as storytellers. As one of many storytellers out there, you must learn to express what those events mean to you and make your characters larger than life.

Here's a useful tip. Brush up on your story images by reading poetry. When you are deep in the throes of your story and you need to take a break and relax, read the poems of Robert Frost, Margaret Atwood, Robert Bly, or other poets of your choice that inspire your imagination. It will do wonders.

I'll let one of the world's great storytellers, who managed to produce more than 600 stories in his lifetime, leave us with this closing thought.

"Try to be original in your story and as clever as possible. Don't be afraid to show yourself foolish; we must have freedom of thinking, and only he who is an emancipated thinker is not afraid to write foolish things. Don't round things out, don't polish --- but be awkward and impudent. Brevity is the sister of talent. Remember, by the way, that declarations of love, the many infidelities of husbands and wives; widows', orphans', and all other tears, have long since been written up in many variations; it is left up for you to find a new approach as a storyteller."

Anton Chekov

Words are all we have. Stay well, keep writing and good luck.

Screenplay Terminology

adaptation A script in which fact or fiction is translated into a presentation suitable for filming.

antagonist The person, element, or force which opposes the central character of a film in his efforts to attain a goal.

anticlimax An inadvertent drop in tension following the climax with additional material dealing with some secondary issue. The cause ordinarily is the writer's failure to recognize the key element of danger which threatens his central character's desire. Once this threat is resolved, the film is over, save for tying up of loose ends in the denouement.

beat A momentary, predesigned pause in an actor's action or delivery of a speech.

business Action introduced in order to build up or reinforce characterization, a sequence, a plot point, or the like.

caper film An adventure film centering on a major theft; generally presented from the thieves' point of view.

character A person in a film.

characterization Any and all details of appearance and behavior devised by a scriptwriter to define a given story person as an individual.

chase Use of pursuit of one character by another to build suspense in a film.

climax The point in a screenplay at which the conflict between the desire and danger reaches its ultimate peak.

commentary Narration for a film, spoken by an off-screen voice in voice-over situations.

complication A new and unanticipated story development that throws the central character/protagonist for a loss where the attaining of his ultimate objective is concerned. In effect, a confrontation, complete with goal, conflict, and disaster.

conflict   The interplay between forces seeking to attain mutually incompatible goals.

confrontation   A unit of conflict and the main structural component of plot. A time-unified clash between opposing forces in which one person or group attempts to attain an immediate goal and another person/group attempts to prevent attainment of said goal, its basic pattern is one of goal-conflict disaster, with disaster representing an outcome which has consequences further endangering the first person/group's desire.

contrast   Comparison of one element (situation, object, person, emotion) with another markedly different.

crisis   A peak in a screenplay's development, brought on by a major threat to the protagonist's chances of attaining his story goal.

denouement   The tying up of a film's loose ends following the climax and during or following the resolution. Here questions are answered, lingering tensions released, an ending given an emotionally satisfying twist, and so on.

deus ex machina   When God or the scriptwriter intercedes with this writing device to save a film from its logical conclusion.

documentary   In general, it refers to a film that avoids artifice and dramatization in favor of extreme realism, shooting in actual settings with non-professional actors who live the parts of the story.

dramatic scene   A confrontation.

empathy   The tendency of viewers to share the experiences of filmed characters, as when they tense at some threat jeopardizing a person in the picture.

exploitation film   A low-budget picture for a specialized audience – horror fans, bikers, or the like.

exposition   Introduction of information from the past necessary for understanding of a film story.

flashback   The introduction into a film of a shot or sequence revealing something from the past, as when a character recalls a past event.

218

French scene   A dramatic unit under a system of designation which decrees a new scene to begin with each non-incidental entrance or exit.

gimmick   A clever plot device, especially one that helps to resolve the film's problem.

hook   A striking incident, unique action, or the like, used to capture audience attention at the beginning of a picture. Or it could be a linking device used to render dialogue cohesive by tying each speech to the one ahead of it.

identification   The tendency of a screenplay's audience to take sides, in effect cheering the hero and booing the villain.

jeopardy   Anything which endangers a character's chances of attaining his story goal and fulfilling his desire.

MacGuffin   A plot device that is not important what object the MacGuffin specifically is. Anything that serves, as a motivation will do while its use can test the suspension of disbelief of audiences since it is not the point of the story.

mise-en-scene   A film's environment. The sum total of its setting.

motivation   The logical basis for a character's action.

muse   The inspiration that supposedly visits, leaves, and suggests things to an artist, especially a poet.

obligatory scene   A film's climatic confrontation, the elements for which have been planted beforehand. Unless these plants are paid off in an appropriate scene, the audience will be frustrated and disappointed.

P.O.V.   An instruction to the cameraman to show the indicated action from the Point-of-View of the character.

pay off   To make significant use of something previously planted, as when at the climax of a film the protagonist faces down the villain with a previously planted pistol.

picaresque   A film – frequently episodic costume drama – which recounts the adventures of a rogue. An example would be the films Tom Jones and Casanova.

plant   Apparently offhand establishment of an idea, character, or property to be used more significantly later in the film. The fact that a gun is seen in a drawer when said drawer is opened later to get a pad or pencil is such an example.

plot   A writer's dramatized plan of action for manipulating audience emotions.

plot line   A line of dialogue essential to development and understanding of the plot, or also known as a film's story line.

predicament   A situation so emotionally disturbing to the central character in a screenplay that he is motivated to take action directed at changing said situation.

premise   A hypothetical 'what if' question that provides the basic idea for, and springboard to, a film story.

progression   Forward movement of a screenplay towards its climax through incorporation of new information and developments.

proportioning   The matching of emphasis to importance in a film script, building some segments large while holding others down.

protagonist   A film's main character; the character in whose fate the audience is most interested.

relief   A sequence or sequences designed to reduce audience tension, sometimes with humor, after a period of high excitement.

resolution   The defeat of desire by danger or visa versa in consequence of the protagonist's behavior in the ultimate conflict that is the climax; the payoff for the hero's trauma; the method of solving the screenplay's main problem.

scenario   A largely obsolete term for a script form giving a general description of the action of a proposed film.

spine   A script's skeletal backbone; its basic plot.

step outline   A sequence outline for a feature or a television film, specifying the action to take place in each sequence as the story develops.

story analyst   A person who appraises and synopsizes potential screenplay material.

story line   A screenplay's main line of devlelopment

story treatment   A semi-dramatized, present tense, preliminary structuring of a screenplay or, more broadly, any script.

structure   A script's framework, its pattern of organization. The combining of story elements into such a pattern.

subplot   A story-within-a-story, generally involving subordinate characters and developed in terms of action parallel to that of the main plot. A subplot's purpose ordinarily is to provide relief from main plot tension.

suspense   Uncertainly of outcome; the fear something will or won't happen.

synopsis   A brief outline of a proposed film's content.

tag line   The final speech in a confrontation, episode, or sequence; generally, one that tops those lines which have gone before.

target audience   The group to which a film is designed to appeal.

tempo   The impression of pace in a film.

theme   A screenplay's implicit message.

transition   The bridge from one confrontation to another. Or anything that links together sequential units or elements in a film.

treatment outline   A third person, present tense summary of a proposed fact film script or, more broadly, any film.

v.o.   Stands for voice-over. This is when dialogue is heard, but the character is not seen.

weenie   An objectification of the hero's desire in simplistic films – and some not so simplistic. The thing sought: the jewels, the formula, and the stolen money.

wank   A mountain in Bavaria, or a person who doesn't finish writing his or her screenplay.

RECOMMENDED READING

The Artists Way by Julia Cameron
Putnam Publishers, 1994

The Hero with a Thousand Faces by Joseph Campbell
Princeton Press, 1968

Myths to Live By by Joseph Campbell
Viking Press, 1972

Adventures in the Screen Trade by William Goldman
Warner Books, 1983

The Screenwriter's Workbook by Syd Field
Dell Publishing, 1984

The Courage to Create by Rollo May
Bantam Books, 1990

The Art of Creative Writing by Lajos Egri
The Citadel Press, 1965

The Screenwriter Looks at the Screenwriter by William Froug
Dell Publishing, 1972

Hitchcock by Francois Truffaut
Panther Books, 1969

Making a Good Script Great by Linda Seger
Dodd Mead, 1987

Hooked by Pauline Kael
E.P. Dutton, 1985

An Actor Prepares by Constantin Stanislavski
Theatre Arts Books, 1970

A Dream of Passion by Lee Strasberg
Penguin Group, 1987

Respect for Acting by Uta Hagen
Wiley Publishing, 1973

Stolen Apples by Yevgeny Yevtushenko
Doubleday Publishing, 1971

Visual Scripting by John Halas
New York: Hastings House, 1976

501 Must Read Books edited by Polly Manguel
Bounty Books, 2006

The Poetry of Robert Frost by Robert Frost
Henry Holt, 1973

Margaret Atwood Poems by Margaret Atwood
Virago Press, 1991

Loving a Woman in Two Worlds by Robert Bly
Harper & Row, 1987

ABOUT THE AUTHOR

Jack McAdam started his career in the entertainment industry with the Canadian Broadcasting Corporation in his native city of Toronto, Canada. While in the Design Department, over a ten year period, Jack designed numerous network dramas, variety shows, operas, and ballets. He lived and worked in Los Angeles for twenty five years, and has several Emmy nominations and awards for his work in both film and television. Jack is a published author and has a number of screenplays, short stories and children's literature to his credit.

In the 1990's Jack was the General Manager of the Mediterranean Film Studios in Malta over a two-year period, where he was responsible for developing new business in the UK, Europe and the Middle East. While operating the studio he had the opportunity of reading dozens of screenplays that needed to be evaluated for production. Jack was instrumental in securing contracts with the Dino DeLaurentiis feature, *U-571* for the German U-Boats that were built and filmed at the studio. He also coordinated the locations in Malta with Ridley Scott for his epic film *Gladiator.*

Jack is a founding member of the Writers Group with the Academy of Television Arts and Sciences in Hollywood, and a member of the Writers Guild of Canada. He has lectured on screenwriting and producing at UCLA, Loyola College, the Hollywood Screen Actors Guild, the University of Malta, the Cinema People's Academy in Bombay, India, and has taught summer writing seminars at the prestigious International Film, Television & Music Academy (IFFMA), in Gauting, Germany. Jack currently resides in Barrie, Ontario, Canada, with his wife Anne, and may be reached by e-mail at: JackMcAdam@Rogers.com

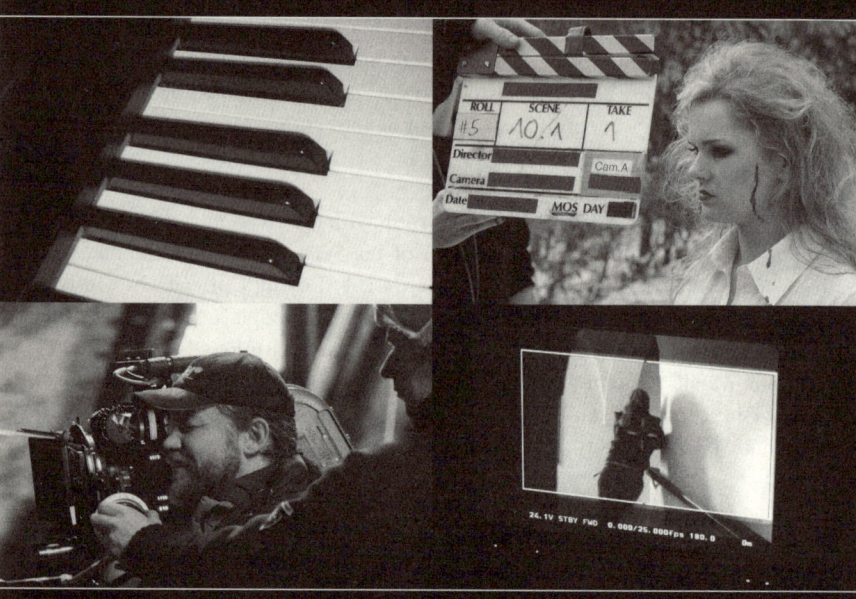
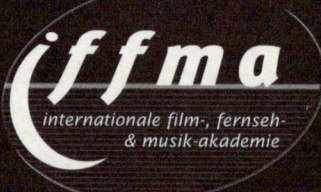